Five Inspiring Essays
by Mystical Thinkers
of the 17th Century

SPIRITUAL PROGRESS

FRANÇOIS **FÉNELON**
MADAME **GUYON**
PÈRE **LACOMBE**

WHITAKER
HOUSE

Spiritual Progress

ISBN: 978-1-60374-969-5
eBook ISBN: 978-1-60374-570-3
Printed in the United States of America

Whitaker House
1030 Hunt Valley Circle
New Kensington, PA 15068
www.whitakerhouse.com

Library of Congress Cataloging-in-Publication Data (pending)

1 2 3 4 5 6 7 8 9 10 11 W 20 19 18 17 16 15 14

CONTENTS

EDITOR'S PREFACE

The providence of God among the churches seems to call to the present time for further light upon the subject of a higher experience than that usually attained by the members of our Christian societies. Among the teachers who have been, from time to time, anointed for this work, François Fénelon and Madame Guyon are justly held in high estimation. While some people, perhaps, have had a more interior experience, few, if any, have so joined to the deepest devotion a power of spiritual analysis that eminently fitted them for the office of instructors.

The extracts from Fénelon given here under the title *Christian Counsel* have been translated from *Avis Chretiens,* contained in the fourth volume of the Paris edition of his works in ten volumes (1810). The *Spiritual Letters* are from the same source.

The translation of the *Method of Prayer* is that which commonly passes under the name of Thomas Digby Brooke. It has been carefully compared and corrected by the editions of the *Opuscules,* published in Cologne (1704) and Paris (1790). *On the Way to God* and *Spiritual Maxims,* which follow, have been translated from the Paris edition of 1790.

It was at first proposed to have prefixed to the selections an account of the lives of the authors, but the design was subsequently abandoned. The very unsatisfactory character of a mere sketch, the space that would be demanded by anything like a fitting biography, and the very accessible form in which the materials have been lately placed by Professor Upham are some of the reasons that contributed to the change.

As this little work is intended to be simply a devotional, matter of a purely sectarian or controversial character has been omitted as far as possible.

And now, beloved reader, one word in conclusion, from the love of God to you. God has led you, in His providence, to open this book that He may do you good. If through His infinite mercy you have had a personal experience of the matters written here, your heart will be filled with thanksgiving and praise as you read. What has God wrought! If not, you will find many things strange, and it would not be surprising if you should be ready to pronounce some things untrue. But beware of being wise in your own conceit! The Spirit of God who searches the deep things of God alone can decide.

Do not distrust the reports of these spies whom God has sent before you into the Promised Land. It is a land flowing with milk and honey; true, the children of Anak are there, in whose sight we are but as grasshoppers, but they are bread for us. The Lord God will fight for us, and He will surely bring us into that exceedingly good land.

The natural man does not receive the things of God, for they are foolishness to him; neither can he know them, because they are spiritually discerned. If, then, you have not experienced the things that follow, do not think it strange that they should seem foolish and false; in God's own time, they will be perceived, if you follow on to know.

If you will be advised by one who knows nothing and who is least in the household of faith, you will deny nothing, reject nothing, and despise nothing, lest you be found fighting against God. You will receive nothing but what is accompanied by the *amen* of the Spirit of God in your heart; all else will be as the idle wind. Reading thus, in absolute dependence, not upon man's wisdom or teaching but upon the utterances of the blessed Spirit within, you will infallibly be guided into all truth. Such is the promise of Him who cannot lie. And may His blessing rest upon you!

Christian Counsel

By François Fénelon

"I counsel thee to buy of me gold tried in the fire, that thou mayest be rich; and white raiment, that thou mayest be clothed, and that the shame of thy nakedness do not appear; and anoint thine eyes with eyesalve, that thou mayest see."

—Revelation 3:18

Contents

1

On the Little Knowledge of God There Is in the World

What men stand most in need of is the knowledge of God. They know, to be sure, by dint of reading, that history gives an account of a certain series of miracles and marked providences. They have reflected seriously on the corruption and instability of worldly things. They are even, perhaps, convinced that the reformation of their lives on certain principles of morality is desirable in order for their salvation. But the whole of the edifice is destitute of foundation; this pious and Christian exterior possesses no soul. The living principle that animates every true believer—God, the All in All, the Author and the Sovereign of all—is wanting.

He is, in all things, infinite—in wisdom, power, and love—and it is no wonder that everything that comes from His hand should partake of the same infinite character and set at naught the efforts of human reason. When God works, His ways and His thoughts are declared by the prophet to be as far above our ways and our thoughts as the heavens are above the earth. (See Isaiah 55:9.) He makes no effort when He would execute what He has decreed, for to Him all things are equally easy. He speaks and causes the heavens and the earth to be created out of nothing with as little difficulty as he causes water or a stone to fall to the ground. His power is co-extensive with His will; when He wills something, it is already accomplished. When the Scriptures represent Him as speaking in the creation of the world, it is not to be understood as signifying that it was necessary that the word of command should issue from Him in order for the universe He was about to create to hear and obey His will; that word was simple and interior, neither more nor less than the thought that He conceived of what He was about to do and the will to do it. The thought was fertile, and without being rendered exterior, it birthed from Him, as the fountain of all life, the sum of the things that are.

His mercy, too, is His pure will. He loved us before the creation of the world; He saw and knew us, and He prepared His blessings for us. He loved and chose us from all eternity. Every new blessing we receive is derived from this eternal origin. He forms no new will respecting us; it is not He who changes but we. When we are righteous and good, we are conformable to His will and agreeable to Him; when we depart from well doing and cease to be good, we cease to be conformable to Him and to please Him. This is the immutable standard that the changeable creature is continually approaching and leaving. God's justice against the wicked and His love toward the righteous are the same thing; it is the same quality that unites Him to everything that is good and is incompatible with everything that is evil. Mercy is the goodness of God, beholding our wickedness and striving to make us good. Perceived by us in time, it has its source in the eternal love of God for His creatures.

From Him alone proceeds true goodness, which is unfortunate for those presumptuous souls who seek it in themselves! It is God's love toward us that gives us everything, but the richest of His gifts is that we may love Him with that love that is His due. When He is able, by His love, to produce that love in us, He reigns within; He constitutes within us our life, our peace, and our happiness; and we then already begin to taste that blissful existence that He enjoys. His love toward us is stamped with His own character of infinity. It is not like ours, bounded and constrained. When He loves, all the measures of His love are infinite. He comes down from heaven to earth to seek the creature of clay whom He loves; He becomes creature and clay with him; He gives him his flesh to eat.

These are the prodigies of divine love in which the infinite exceeds all the affection we can manifest. He loves like a God, with a love utterly incomprehensible. It is the height of folly to seek to measure infinite love by human wisdom. Far from losing any element of its greatness in these excesses, He impresses upon His love the stamp of His own grandeur, while He manifests a delight in us that is bounded by only the infinite. How great and lovely He is in His mysteries! But we lack eyes to see them and have no desire to behold God in everything.

2

On the Necessity of Knowing and Loving God

It is not astonishing that men do so little for God and that the little that they do costs them so much. They do not know Him; scarcely do they believe that He exists, and the impression they have of Him is more of a blind deference for general opinion than a lively and distinct conviction of the Divinity. They suppose it is so because they do not dare to examine and because they are indifferent in the matter, their souls being distracted by the inclination of their affections and passions for other objects. But their only idea of Him is of something wonderful, far off and unconnected with us. They think of Him as a stern and powerful being who is ever making requisitions upon us, thwarting our inclinations, threatening us with great evils, and against whose terrible judgment it behooves everyone to be on his or her guard.

Such is the inward thought of those who think seriously about religion, and their number even is small enough. "He is one who fears God," they say. And in truth, such a person fears only; he does not love. He is as the child who is in awe of the master who punishes him or as the servant who dreads the blows of the one whom he serves from fear, and of whose interests he is utterly regardless. Would he like to be treated by a son or a servant as he treats God? It is because God is not known; if He were known, He would be loved. "*God is love*" (1 John 4:8; see also John 4:16), says the apostle John. The person who does not love Him, does not know Him, for how could he know love without loving Him? It is plain, then, that all those who have previously only feared God have not known Him.

But who will know You, O my God? He who will seek with his whole heart to know You and who will know himself with approbation no longer. The person to whom all that is not, You will be as though it were! The world cannot receive this saying because the world is full of self, vanity, and lies, and is empty of God, but I trust that there will always be souls hungering for God; those who will relish the truth that I am about to set forth.

O my God, before You made the heavens and the earth, there was none other but You. You were, because Your years have no beginning; but You were alone. Outside of You, there was nothing, and You did rejoice in this blessed solitude. You are all sufficient in Yourself, and You had no need of anything outside of Yourself, for none can give to You, and it is You who gives to all by Your all-powerful Word, that is, by Your simple will. To it, nothing is difficult, and it does whatever it will from its own labor. You caused this world, which had not yet been formed, to begin to be—but not as the workmen of the earth, who find the materials for their work ready-made in their hands and whose art consists of bringing these materials together and arranging them by slow degrees in the requisite order. You found nothing ready-made, but created all the materials for Your work. It was to nothing that You said, "Let the world be," and it was. You only needed to speak, and it was done.

But why did You create all of these things? They were all made for man, and man was made for You. This is the order of Your appointment. Woe to the one who inverts it, who believes that all should be for him and shuts himself in self! He breaks the fundamental law of creation.

No, Lord, You cannot yield the essential prerogatives of a creator; it would degrade You. You can pardon the guilty soul who has warred against You, because You can fill him with Your pure love; but You cannot cease to be at variance with the soul who refers all of Your gifts to himself and refuses to embrace You as his Creator with a sincere and disinterested affection.

To have no feeling but fear is not to refer himself to You, but on the contrary, it is to think of You solely with reference to self. To love You with a single eye to the good You can bestow is not to lose oneself in You but to lose You in self! What, then, must be done in order that we may be lost in You? We must renounce, forget, and forever lose sight of self; then we must take part with You, and shine, O God, against ourselves and ours. We must no longer have any will, glory, or peace, except Yours only; in a word, we must love You without loving self, except as it is in and for You.

God, who made us out of nothing, re-creates us, as it were, every moment. It does not follow that because we were alive yesterday, we will of course be alive today; we would cease to exist and return to the nothingness out of which He formed us unless the same all-powerful hand prevented it. Of ourselves, we are nothing; we are but what God has made us, and only for as long as He pleases. He has only to withdraw His hand, which sustains us, and we plunge into an abyss of annihilation, as a stone held in the air falls by its own weight when its support is removed. Existence and life, then, are only ours because they are conferred by God.

There are blessings, however, of a purer and higher order than these. A well-ordered life is better than life; virtue is of higher price than health; uprightness of heart and the love of God are as far above temporal goods as the heavens are above the earth. If, then, these lower and baser gifts are held only through the mercy and at the pleasure of God, how much more this must be true of the sublime gift of His love!

They know You not, then, O my God, who regard You as an all-powerful Being who is separate from themselves, who gives laws to all nature, and who is creator of everything we behold. They know You but in part! They know not that which is most marvelous and which most nearly concerns Your rational creatures!

To know that You are the God of my heart, that You do there what pleases You, is what elevates and affects me! When I am good, it is because You render me so. Not only do You turn my heart as You please, but You give me a heart like Your own! It is Yourself that You love in me. You are the life of my soul as my soul is the life of my body. You are more intimately present to me than I am to myself. This self, to which I am so attached, and which I have so ardently loved, ought to be strange to me in comparison with You. You are the One who bestows it; without You, it never would have been. Therefore, You desire that I would love You better than I love myself.

O the incomprehensible power of my Creator! O the rights of the Creator over the creature that the creature will never sufficiently comprehend! O the prodigy of love that God alone could perform! God interposes Himself, as it were, between me and myself. He separates me from myself. In His pure love, He desires to be nearer to me than I am to myself. He would have me look upon this "me" as a stranger; He would have me escape from its walls and sacrifice it wholly to Him, returning it absolutely and unconditionally to Him from whom I received it. What I am should certainly be less precious to me than the One by whom I am. He made me for Himself and not to be my own, that is, to love Him and to will what He wills and to not seek my own will. Does anyone feel his heart revolt at this total sacrifice of self to the One who has created us? I weep for his blindness; I feel compassion for his bondage to self and pray that God delivers him from it by teaching him to love Him above every other object.

O my God, in these souls, who are offended at Your pure love, I behold the darkness and rebellion resulting from the fall! You did not make man's heart will this monstrous passion of appropriation. The Scriptures teach us that the uprightness that he was originally created in consisted in this—that he had no claim upon himself but acknowledged that he belonged to his Creator. O Father, Your children are sadly changed and no longer bear Your image! They are enraged; they are discouraged when they are told that they should belong to You as You belong to Yourself! They desire to reverse this holy order and would madly elevate themselves into gods. They desire to be their own god, to do everything for themselves or, at least, to surrender themselves with certain reservations and conditions and for their own advantage. O monstrous usurpation! O unknown rights of God! O the ingratitude and insolence of the creature! Miserable nothing!

What have you to keep for yourself! What have you that belongs to you? What have you that did not come from on high and that ought not return there? Everything, yes, even this self, which seeks to divide God's gifts from God, is a gift of God and was made only for Him. Everything within you cries out against you and for your Creator. Be still, then, you who, having been created, would deny your Creator; and instead, surrender yourself wholly to Him.

But alas, O my God, what a consolation it is to know that everything within me, as well as outside of me, is the work of Your hand! You are ever with me. When I do wrong, You are within me, reproaching me with the evil that I do, raising within me regrets for the good that I abandon, and opening to me Your arms of mercy. When I do good, You inspire the desire and do it in me and with me; it is You who loves good and hates evil in my heart, who suffers and prays, who does good to the neighbor and gives alms. I do all these things only by Your means. You cause me to do them;

it is You who puts them in me. These good works, which are Your gifts, become my works, but they do not cease to be Your gifts. But they do cease to be good works if I look at them for a moment as emanating from myself or if I forget that they are good only because they come from You.

You, then, are incessantly working within me (it is my delight to believe it!); there You labor invisibly like a miner in the bowels of the earth. You do everything, and yet the world beholds You not and attributes nothing to You. Even I wandered everywhere vainly searching for You outside of myself; I ran over all the wonders of nature that I might form some conception of Your greatness; I asked Your creatures about You and not once thought of finding You in the depths of my heart, where You have never ceased to dwell. No, O my God, it is not necessary to descend into the depths or to pass beyond the seas; it is not necessary to ascend into the heavens to find You. You are nearer to us than we are to ourselves.

O my God, who is at once so great and so condescending, so high above the heavens and so accommodating to the misery of the creature, so infinite and so intimately enclosed in the depths of my heart, so terrible and so lovely, so jealous and so easily entreated by those who converse with You with the familiarity of pure love—when will Your children cease to be ignorant of You? Where will I find a voice loud enough to reproach the whole world with its blindness and to tell it with authority all that You are? When we bid men look for You in their own hearts, it is as though we bade them search for You in the remotest and most unknown lands! What territory is more distant or more unknown to them, vain and dissipated as they are, than the ground of their own hearts? Do they even know what it is to enter within themselves? Have they ever endeavored to find the way? Can they even form the most distant conception of the nature of that interior sanctuary, that impenetrable depth of the soul, where You desire to be worshipped in spirit and in truth? (See John 4:24.) They are ever outside of themselves in the objects of their ambition or their pleasure. Alas, how can they understand heavenly truths, since, as our Lord says, they cannot even comprehend those that are earthly? (See John 3:12.) They cannot conceive what it is to enter within themselves by serious reflection. What would they say if they were told to come out of themselves so that they might be lost in God?

As for me, my Creator, I shut my eyes to all exterior things, which are but vanity and vexation of spirit (see Ecclesiastes 1:14) so that I may enjoy in the deepest recesses of my heart an intimate companionship with You through Jesus Christ, Your Son, who is Your wisdom and eternal understanding. He became a child so that by His childhood and the folly of His cross He might put to shame our vain and lying wisdom. Cost what it may, and in spite of my fears and speculations, I desire to become lowly and a fool, still more despicable in my own eyes than in the eyes of the wise in their own conceit. Like the apostles, I would become drunk with the Holy Spirit and be content with them to become the sport of the world.

I find You everywhere within me. It is You who does every good thing I seem to do. I have a thousand times experienced that I could not of myself govern my temper, overcome my habits, subdue my pride, follow my reason, or will again the good that I once willed. It is You who must both bestow the will and preserve it pure; without You, I am but a reed shaken by the wind. You are the Author of all the courage, uprightness, and truth that I possess. You have given me a new heart that longs after Your righteousness and is thirsty for Your eternal truth. You have taken away the old man full of filth and corruption, which was jealous, vain, ambitious, restless, unrighteous, and devoted to its own pleasure. In what a state of misery did I live. Ah! Could I ever have believed that I would be able in this way to turn to You and shake off the yoke of my tyrannical passions?

But behold a marvel that eclipses all the rest! Who but You could ever have snatched me from myself and turned all my hatred and contempt against mine own bosom? I have not done this, for it is not by our own power that we depart from self. No! You, O Lord, shone with Your own light into the depths of my heart, which could not be reached by any other, and there You revealed the whole of my foulness. I know that, even after beholding, I have not changed it—that I am still filthy in Your sight, that my eyes have not been able to discover the extent of my pollution. But I have, at least, seen a part, and I desire to behold the whole. I am despised in my own sight, but the hope that I have in You causes me to live in peace, for I will neither flatter my defects nor allow them to discourage me. I take Your side, O God, against myself; it is only by Your strength that I am able to do this. Behold what God has wrought within me! And You continue Your work from day to day in cleansing me from the old Adam and in building up the new. This is the new creation that is gradually going on.

I leave myself, Father, in your hands. Make and remake this clay; shape it or grind it to atoms. It is Your own; it has nothing to say. Only let it always be subservient to Your ever-blessed designs, and let nothing in me oppose Your good pleasure for which I was created. Require, command, forbid—what would You have me do? What would you have me not do? Exalted or abased, rejoicing or suffering, doing Your work or laying it aside, I will always praise You alike, ever yielding up all my own will to Yours! Nothing remains for me but to adopt the language of Mary: *"Be it unto me according to thy word"* (Luke 1:38).

Let me, O my God, stifle forever in my heart every thought that would tempt me to doubt Your goodness. I know that You cannot be anything but good. O merciful Father, let me no longer reason about grace but silently abandon myself to its operation. Grace performs everything in us but does it with and through us; it is by grace, therefore, that I act, that I forbear, that I suffer, that I wait, that I resist, that I believe, that I hope, and that I love—all in cooperation with grace. Following its guidance, it will do all things in me, and I shall do all things through it. It moves the heart, but the heart must act; there is no salvation without man's action. I must work, then, without losing a moment so that I may put no hindrance in the way of that grace that is incessantly working within me. All the good is of grace; all the evil is of self. When I do right, it is grace that does it; when I do wrong, it is because I resist grace. I pray, God, that I may not seek to know more than this; all else will but serve to nourish a presumptuous curiosity. O my God, keep me ever in the number of those children to whom You reveal Your mysteries while You conceal them from the wise and prudent!

You cause me clearly to understand that You make use of the evils and imperfections of the creature to do the good that You have determined beforehand. You conceal Yourself under the importunate visitor who intrudes upon the occupation of Your impatient child so that he may learn not to be impatient and that he may die to the gratification of being free to study or work as he pleases. You avail Yourself of slanderous tongues to destroy the reputation of Your innocent children so that, beside their innocence, they may offer You the sacrifice of their too highly cherished reputation. By the cunning artifices of the envious, You lay low the fortunes of those who were too much set upon their prosperity. It is Your hand that sends death upon him to whom life is a constant source of danger and the tomb a harbor of refuge. It is You who makes his death a remedy—bitter enough, it is true, but effectual—for those who were too fondly attached to him. Thus, while saving one by removing him from life, You prepare the others, by that very act, for a happy death. Thus You mercifully strew bitterness over everything that is not Yourself, to the end that our hearts, formed to love You and to exist upon Your love, may be, as it were, constrained to return to You by a want of satisfaction in everything else.

And this is because You are all love, and consequently all jealousy. O jealous God (for thus You are called), a divided heart displeases You; a wandering one excites Your pity. You are infinite in all things, in love as well as in wisdom and power. You love like an infinite God when You love; You move heaven and earth to save Your loved ones. You became a man, a babe, the vilest of men, covered with reproaches, dying with infamy and under the pangs of the cross. All this is not too much for an infinite love. Our finite love and limited wisdom cannot understand it. How should the finite comprehend the infinite? It has neither eyes to see it nor a heart to take it in. The debased and narrowed soul of man and his vain wisdom are offended and can perceive no trace of God in this excess of love. But for myself, it is by this very character of infinity that I recognize it. This is the love that does all things, that brings to pass even the evils we suffer, so shaping them that they are but the instruments of preparing the good that, as of yet, has not arrived.

But, ah, when will we return love for love? When will we seek Him who seeks us and constantly carries us in His arms? When He bears us along in His tender and paternal bosom, then we forget Him. In the sweetness of His gifts, we forget the Giver. His ceaseless blessings, instead of melting us into love, distract our attention and turn it away from Him.

3

On Pure Love

Scripture says, *"The* Lord *hath made all things for himself"* (Proverbs 16:4). Everything belongs to Him, and He will never release His right to anything. Free and intelligent creatures are His as much as those that are otherwise. He refers every unintelligent thing totally and absolutely to Himself, and He desires that His intelligent creatures should voluntarily make the same disposition of themselves. It is true that He desires our happiness, but that is neither the chief end of His work nor an end to be compared with that of His glory. It is for His glory only that He wills our happiness; the latter is a subordinate consideration, which He refers to the final and essential end of His glory.

That we may enter into His designs in this respect, we must prefer God before ourselves and endeavor to will our own happiness for His glory; in any other case, we invert the order of things. And we must not desire His glory on account of our own salvation, but on the other hand, the desire for His glory should impel us to seek our own happiness as a thing that He has been pleased to make a part of His glory. It is true that not all holy souls are capable of exercising this explicit preference for God over themselves, but there must at least be an implicit preference. The former, which is more perfect, is reserved for those whom God has endowed with light and strength to prefer Him to themselves, to such a degree as to desire their own happiness simply because it adds to His glory.

Men have a great repugnance to this truth and consider it to be a very hard saying, because they are lovers of self from self-interest. They understand, in a general and superficial way, that they must love God more than all His creatures, but they have no conception of loving God more than themselves and loving themselves only for Him. They can utter these great words without difficulty because they do not enter into their meaning, but they shudder when it is explained to them that God and His glory are to be preferred before ourselves and everything else to such a degree that we must love His glory more than our own happiness and must refer the latter to the former, as a subordinate means to an end.

4

On Prayer and the Principal Exercises of Piety

True prayer is another name for the love of God. Its excellence does not consist in the multitude of our words, for our Father knows what things we have need of before we ask Him. The true prayer is that of the heart, and the heart prays only for what it desires. To *pray*, then, is to *desire*—but to desire what God would have us desire. He who asks what he does not from the bottom of his heart desire is mistaken in thinking that he prays. Let him spend days in reciting prayers, in meditation, or in inciting himself to pious exercises; he prays not once truly if he does not really desire the things he pretends to ask.

O how few there are who pray! For how few are those who desire what is truly good! Crosses, external and internal humiliation, renouncement of our own wills, the death of ourselves, and the establishment of God's throne upon the ruins of self love—these are indeed good. Not to desire these is not to pray; to desire them seriously, soberly, constantly, and with reference to all the details of life is true prayer. Not to desire them, and yet to suppose we pray, is an illusion like that of the wretched who dream themselves happy. Alas, how many souls full of self and an imaginary desire for perfection in the midst of hosts of voluntary imperfections have never yet uttered this true prayer of the heart! It is in reference to this that Saint Augustine says, "He that loveth little, prayeth little; he that loveth much, prayeth much."

On the other hand, that heart in which the true love of God and true desire exists never ceases to pray. Love, hidden in the bottom of the soul, prays without ceasing, even when the mind is drawn another way. God continually beholds the desire that He has Himself implanted in the soul, though it may at times be unconscious of its existence. His heart is touched by it; it ceaselessly attracts His mercies. It is that Spirit that, according to Saint Paul, helps our infirmities and makes intercession for us with groanings that cannot be uttered. (See Romans 8:26.)

Love desires of God that He would give us what we need and that He would have less regard for our frailty than for the purity of our intentions. It even covers over our trifling defects and purifies us like a consuming fire. *"He maketh intercession for the saints according to the will of God"* (Romans 8:27), *"for we know not what we should pray for as we ought"* (Romans 8:26); in our ignorance, we frequently request what would be injurious. We should like fervor of devotion, distinct sensible joys, and apparent perfections, which would serve to nourish within us the life of self and a confidence in our own strength; but love leads us on, abandons us to all the operations of grace, puts us entirely at the disposal of God's will, and thus prepares us for all His secret designs.

Then we will all things and yet nothing. What God gives is precisely what we should have desired to ask, for we will whatever He wills and only that. Thus, this state contains all prayer; it is a work of the heart that includes all desire. The Spirit prays within us for those very things that the Spirit Himself wills to give us. Even when we are occupied with outward things and our thoughts are drawn off by the providential engagements of our position, we still carry within us a constantly burning fire, which not only cannot be extinguished but also nourishes a secret prayer and is as a lamp continually lighted before the throne of God. *"I sleep, but my heart waketh"* (Song of Solomon 5:2). *"Blessed are those servants, whom the lord when he cometh, shall find watching"* (Luke 12:37).

There are two principal points of attention necessary for the preservation of this constant spirit of prayer that unites us with God: We must continually seek to cherish it, and we must avoid everything that tends to make us lose it.

In order to cherish it, we should pursue a regulated course of reading; we must have appointed seasons of secret prayer and frequent states of recollection during the day; we should make use of retirement when we feel the need of it or when it is advised by those of greater experience; and we should unite in the ordinances appropriate to our condition. We should greatly fear and be exceedingly cautious to avoid all things that have a tendency to make us lose this state of prayer. Thus, we should decline those worldly occupations and associates that dissipate the mind, pleasures that excite the passions, and everything calculated to awaken the love of the world and those old inclinations that have caused us so much trouble.

There is an infinity of detail in these two heads; general directions only can be given, because each individual case presents features peculiar to itself.

We should choose those works for reading that instruct us in our duty and in our faults, those that, while they point out the greatness of God, teach us what is our duty to Him and how very far we are from performing it, not those barren productions that melt and sentimentalize the heart. *The tree must bear fruit*; we can only judge of the life of the root by its fecundity.

The first effect of a sincere love is an earnest desire to know all that we ought to do to gratify the object of our affection. Any other desire is a proof that we love ourselves under a pretence of loving God, that we are seeking an empty and deceitful consolation in Him, that we would use God as an instrument for our pleasure instead of sacrificing that for His glory. God forbid that His children should so love Him! Cost what it may, we must both know and do without reservation what He requires of us.

Seasons of secret prayer must be regulated by the leisure, the disposition, the condition, and the inward impulse of each individual.

Meditation is not prayer, but it is its necessary foundation; it brings to mind the truths that God has revealed. We should be conversant not only with all the mysteries of Jesus Christ and the truths of His gospel but also with everything they ought to operate in us for our regeneration. We should be colored and penetrated by them as wool is by the dye.

So familiar should they become to us that, in consequence of seeing them at all times and ever near to us, we may acquire the habit of forming no judgment except in their light, so that they may be to us our only guide in matters of practice, as the rays of the sun are our only light in matters of perception.

When these truths are once, as it were, incorporated in us, then our praying begins to be real and fruitful. Up to that point, it was but a shadow; we thought we had penetrated to the inmost recesses of the gospel when we had barely set foot upon the vestibule—all our most tender and lively feelings, all our firmest resolutions, all our clearest and furthest views were but the rough and shapeless mass from which God would hew in us His likeness.

When His celestial rays begin to shine within us, then we see in the true light; then there is no truth to which we do not instantaneously assent, as we admit, without any process of reasoning, the splendor of the sun the moment we behold his rising beams.

Our union with God must be the result of our faithfulness in doing and suffering all His will.

Our meditations should become every day deeper and more interior. I say *deeper* because by frequent and humble meditation upon God's truth, we penetrate further and further in search of new treasures; and *more interior* because as we sink more and more to enter into these truths, they also descend to penetrate the very substance of our souls. Then it is that a simple word goes further than whole sermons.

The very things that had been fruitlessly and coldly heard a hundred times before now nourishes the soul with a hidden manna, having an infinite variety of flavors for days in succession. Let us beware, too, of ceasing to meditate upon truths that, up to this time, have been blessed to us, so long as there remains any nourishment in them, so long as they yet yield us anything. It is a certain sign that we still need their ministration. We derive instruction from them without receiving any precise or distinct impression. There is an indescribable something in them that helps us more than all our reasoning. We behold a truth; we love it and repose upon it; it strengthens our souls and detaches us from ourselves. Let us dwell upon it in peace as long as possible.

As to the manner of meditating, it should not be subtle or composed of long reasoning; all that is required are simple and natural reflections derived immediately from the subject of our thoughts. We need to take a few truths and meditate upon these without hurry, without effort, and without seeking for far-fetched reflections. Every truth should be considered with reference to its practical bearing. To receive it without employing all means to put it faithfully into practice at whatever cost is to desire to *"hold the truth in unrighteousness"* (Romans 1:18). It is a resistance to the truth impressed upon us and, of course, to the Holy Spirit. This is the most terrible of all unfaithfulness.

As to a method of prayer, each one must be guided by his own experience. Those who find themselves profited in using a strict method need not depart from it, while those who cannot so confine themselves may make use of their own mode without ceasing to respect that which has been useful to many and which so many pious and experienced persons have highly recommended. A method is intended to assist; if it be found to embarrass, instead of assisting, the sooner it is discarded the better.

The most natural mode, at first, is to take a book and to cease reading it whenever we feel so inclined by the passage with which we are engaged, and, whenever that no longer ministers to our interior nourishment, to begin again. As a general rule, those truths that we highly relish and that shed a degree of practical light upon the things we are required to give up for God are leadings of divine grace that we should follow without hesitation. "*The wind* [Spirit] *bloweth where it listeth*" (John 3:8); "*and where the Spirit of the Lord is, there is liberty*" (2 Corinthians 3:17).

In the course of time, the proportion of reflections and reasoning will diminish and that of tender feelings, affecting views, and desires will increase as we become sufficiently instructed and convinced by the Holy Spirit. The heart is satisfied, nourished, warmed, and set on fire; a word will give it only employment for a long time.

Finally, increase of prayer is indicated by an increase of simplicity and steadiness in our views, a great multitude of objects and considerations being no longer necessary. Our intercourse with God resembles that with a friend; at first, there are a thousand things to be told and as many things to be asked; but after a time, these diminish, while the pleasure of being together does not. Everything has been said, but the satisfaction of seeing each other, of feeling that one is near the other or reposing in the enjoyment of a pure and sweet friendship, can be felt without conversation;

the silence is eloquent and mutually understood. Each party feels that the other is in perfect sympathy with him, and that their two hearts are incessantly poured—one into the other—and constitute but one.

Thus it is that in prayer, our communion with God becomes a simple and familiar union, far beyond the need of words. But let it be remembered that God Himself must alone institute this prayer within us; nothing would be more rash or more dangerous than to dare to attempt it by ourselves. We must suffer ourselves to be led step-by-step by someone conversant with the ways of God, who may lay the immovable foundations of correct teaching and the complete death of self in everything.

In regard to retirement and attending upon ordinances, we must be governed by the advice of someone in whom we have confidence. Our own necessities, the effect produced upon us, and many other circumstances are to be taken into consideration.

Our leisure and our needs must regulate our retirements. Our *needs*, because it is with the soul as it is with the body; when we can no longer work without nourishment, we must take it; we will otherwise be in danger of fainting. Our *leisure*, because, this absolute necessity of food excepted, we must attend to duty before we seek enjoyment in spiritual exercises. The man who has public duties and spends the time appropriate to them in meditating in retirement would miss of God while he was seeking to be united to Him. True union with God is to do His will without ceasing, in spite of all our natural disinclination and in every duty of life, however disagreeable or mortifying.

As precautions against wanderings, we must avoid close and intimate intercourse with those who are not pious, especially when we have been before led astray by their infectious maxims. (See Proverbs 13:20.) They will open our wounds afresh. They have a secret correspondence deep in our souls; there is there a soft and insinuating counselor who is always ready to blind and deceive us.

"Would you judge of a man?" asks the Holy Spirit. Observe who his companions are. How can the one who loves God and who loves nothing except in and for God enjoy the intimate companionship of those who neither love nor know God and who look upon love of Him as a weakness? Can a heart full of God and sensible of its own frailty ever rest and be at ease with those who have no feelings in common with it but are ever seeking to rob it of its treasure? Their delights, and the pleasures of which faith is the source, are incompatible.

I am well aware that we cannot—nay, that we ought not—break with those friends to whom we are bound by esteem of their natural amiability, by their services, by the tie of sincere friendship, or by the regard consequent upon mutual good offices. Friends whom we have treated with a certain familiarity and confidence would be wounded to the quick were we to separate from them entirely. We must gently and imperceptibly diminish our intercourse with them without abruptly declaring our alteration of sentiment. We may see them in private, distinguish them from our less intimate friends, and confide to them those matters in which their integrity and friendship enable them to give us good advice and to think with us, although our reasons for so thinking are more pure and elevated than theirs. In short, we may continue to serve them and to manifest all the attentions of a cordial friendship without suffering our hearts to be embarrassed by them.

How perilous is our state without this precaution! If we do not, from the first, boldly adopt all measures to render our piety entirely free and independent of our unregenerate friends, it is threatened with a speedy downfall. If a man surrounded by such companions be of a yielding disposition and inflammable passions, it is certain that his friends, even the well-intentioned ones, will lead him astray. They may be good, honest, faithful, and possessed of all those qualities that render friendship perfect in the eyes of the world, but for him they are infected, and their amiability only increases the danger. Those who do not have this estimable character should be sacrificed at once; blessed are we when a sacrifice that ought to cost us so little may avail to give us so precious a security for our eternal salvation!

Not only, then, should we be exceedingly careful whom we see, but we must also reserve the necessary time that we may see God alone in prayer. Those who have stations of importance to fill have generally so many indispensable duties to perform that, without the greatest care in the management of their time, none will be left to be alone with God. If they have ever so little inclination for dissipation, the hours that belong to God and their neighbor disappear altogether.

We must be firm in observing our rules. This strictness seems excessive, but without it, everything falls into confusion; we become dissipated, relaxed, and lose strength; we insensibly separate ourselves from God, surrender ourselves to all our pleasures, and only then begin to perceive that we have wandered—when it is almost hopeless to think of endeavoring to return.

Prayer, prayer—this is our only safety. "*Blessed be God, which hath not turned away my prayer, nor his mercy from me*" (Psalm 66:20). And in order to be faithful in prayer, it is indispensable that we dispose all the employments of the day with a regularity nothing can disturb.

5

On Conformity to the Life of Jesus Christ

We must imitate Jesus—live as He lived, think as He thought, and be conformed to His image, which is the seal of our sanctification.

What a contrast! Nothingness strives to be something, and the Omnipotent becomes nothing! I will be nothing with You, my Lord! I offer You the pride and vanity that have possessed me. Help my will; remove from me occasions of my stumbling. *"Turn away mine eyes from beholding vanity"* (Psalm 119:37), and let me behold nothing but You and myself in Your presence, that I may understand what I am and what You are.

Jesus Christ was born in a stable; He was obliged to flee into Egypt; He spent thirty years of His life in a workshop; and He suffered hunger, thirst, and weariness; He was poor, despised, and miserable; He taught the doctrines of heaven, but no one would listen. The great and the wise persecuted and took Him, subjected Him to frightful torments, treated Him as a slave, and put Him to death between two malefactors, having preferred to give liberty to a robber rather than to suffer Christ to escape. Such was the life that our Lord chose, while we are horrified at any kind of humiliation, and cannot bear the slightest appearance of contempt.

Let us compare our lives with that of Jesus Christ, reflecting on the knowledge that He was the Master and that we are the servants, that He was all-powerful and that we are but weakness, that He was abased and that we are exalted. Let us so constantly bear our wretchedness in mind that we may have nothing but contempt for ourselves. With what face can we despise others and dwell upon their faults when we ourselves are filled with nothing else? Let us begin to walk in the path that our Savior has marked out, for it is the only one that can lead us to Him.

And how can we expect to find Jesus if we do not seek Him in the states of His earthly life, in loneliness and silence, in poverty and suffering, in persecution and contempt, in annihilation and the cross? The saints find Him in heaven, in the splendors of glory and in unspeakable pleasures, but they enjoy this only after having dwelt with Him on earth in reproaches, in pain, and in humiliation. To be a Christian is to be an imitator of Jesus Christ. In what can we imitate Him if not in His humiliation? Nothing else can bring us near to Him. We may adore Him as omnipotent, fear Him as just, love Him with all our hearts as good and merciful; but we can only imitate Him as humble, submissive, poor, and despised servants.

Let us not imagine that we can do this by our own efforts; everything that is written is opposed to it. But we may rejoice in the presence of God. Jesus has chosen to be made partaker of all our weaknesses; He is a compassionate high priest who has voluntarily submitted Himself to be tempted in all points as we are. Let us, then, have all our strength in Him who became weak that He might strengthen us; let us enrich ourselves out of His poverty, confidently exclaiming, *"I can do all things through Christ which strengtheneth me"* (Philippians 4:13).

Let me follow in Your footsteps, O Jesus! I would imitate You, but I cannot without the aid of Your grace! O humble and lowly Savior, grant me the knowledge of the true Christian so that I may willingly despise myself; let me learn the lesson, so incomprehensible to the mind of man, that I must die to myself by an abandonment that will produce true humility.

Let us earnestly engage in this work, and change our hard hearts, so rebellious to the heart of Jesus Christ. Let us make some approaches toward the holy soul of Jesus; let Him animate our souls and destroy all our repugnance. O lovely Jesus, who has suffered so many injuries and reproaches for my sake, let me esteem and love them for You, and let me desire to share Your life of humiliation!

6

On Humility

What a mercy is humiliation to a soul who receives it with steadfast faith! There are a thousand blessings in it for us and for others, for our Lord bestows His grace upon the humble. Humility renders us charitable toward our neighbor; nothing will make us as tender and indulgent to the faults of others as a view of our own.

Two things produce humility when combined: the first is a sight of the abyss of wretchedness from which the all-powerful hand of God has snatched us and over which He still holds us, as it were, suspended in the air; and the other is the presence of God, who is *all*.

Our faults, even those most difficult to bear, will all be of service to us if we make use of them for our humiliation without relaxing our efforts to correct them. It does no good to be discouraged; it is the result of a disappointed and despairing self-love. The true method of profiting by the humiliation of our faults is to behold them in all their deformity, without losing our hope in God and without having any confidence in ourselves.

We must bear with ourselves without either flattery or discouragement, a mean seldom attained, for we either expect great things of ourselves and of our good intentions, or wholly despair. We must hope for nothing from self, but wait for everything from God. Utter despair of ourselves, in consequence of a conviction of our helplessness, and unbounded confidence in God, are the true foundations of the spiritual edifice.

That is a false humility, which, acknowledging itself unworthy of the gifts of God, dares not confidently expect them. True humility consists of a deep view of our utter unworthiness and in an absolute abandonment to God, without the slightest doubt that He will do the greatest things in us.

Those who are truly humble will be surprised to hear anything exalted of themselves. They are mild and peaceful, of a contrite and humble heart, and are merciful and compassionate; they are quiet, cheerful, obedient, watchful, fervent in spirit, and incapable of strife; they always take the lowest place, rejoice when they are despised, and consider everyone superior to themselves; they are lenient to the faults of others in view of their own and are very far from preferring themselves before anyone else. We may judge our advancement in humility by the delight we have in humiliations and contempt.

7

On Prayer

Many are tempted to believe that they no longer pray when they cease to enjoy a certain pleasure in the act of prayer. But if they will understand that perfect prayer is only another name for love of God, they will not be deceived.

Prayer, then, does not consist in sweet feelings or in the charms of an excited imagination or in that illumination of the intellect that traces with ease the most sublime truths in God or even in a certain consolation in the view of God. All of these things are external gifts from His hand, in the absence of which love may exist even more purely, as the soul may then attach itself immediately and solely to God instead of to His mercies.

This is that love by naked faith that is the death of nature, because it leaves it no support; and when we are convinced that all is lost, that very conviction is the evidence that all is gained.

Pure love is in the will alone; it is not sentimental love, for the imagination has no part in it. It loves, if we may so express it, without feeling, as faith believes without seeing. We need not fear that this love is an imaginary thing—nothing can be less so than the mere will separate from all imagination. The more purely intellectual and spiritual are the operations of our minds, the nearer they are not only to reality but to the perfection that God requires of us. Their working is more perfect; faith is in full exercise while humility is preserved.

Such love is chaste, for it is the love of God in and for God. We are attached to Him, but not for the pleasure that He bestows on us; we follow Him, but not for the loaves and the fishes.

"What!" some may say. "Can it be that a simple will to be united with God is the whole of piety? How can we be assured that this will is not a mere idea, a trick of the imagination instead of a true willing of the soul?"

I should indeed believe that it was a deception, if it were not the parent of faithfulness on all proper occasions; for a good tree brings forth good fruit, and a true will makes us sincerely earnest and diligent in doing the will of God; but it is still compatible in this life with little failings that are permitted by God that the soul may be humbled. If, then, we experience only these little daily frailties, let us not be discouraged, but extract from them their proper fruit—humility.

True virtue and pure love reside in the will alone. Is it not a great matter to always desire the Supreme Good whenever He is seen; to keep the mind steadily turned toward Him and to bring it back whenever it is perceived to wander; to will nothing advisedly but according to His order; in short, in the absence of all sensible enjoyment, to remain the same in the spirit of a submissive, irreclaimable burnt offering? Do you think it is nothing to repress all the uneasy reflections of self-love; to press forward continually without knowing where we go, and yet without stopping; to cease from self-satisfied thoughts of self or (at least) to think of ourselves as we would of another; to fulfill the indications of Providence for the moment and no further? Is this not more likely to be the death of the Old Adam than fine sentiments, in which we are, in fact, thinking only of ourselves or external acts in the performance of which we congratulate ourselves on our advancement?

It is a sort of infidelity to simple faith when we desire to be continually assured that we are doing well; it is, in fact, to desire to know what we are doing, which we will never know, and of which it is the will of God that we should be ignorant. It is trifling by the way in order to reason about the way. The safest and shortest course is to renounce, forget, and abandon self and, through faithfulness to God, to think no more of it. This is the whole of religion—to get out of self and self-love in order to get in to God.

As to involuntary wanderings, they are no hindrance to love, inasmuch as love is in the will, and the will only wanders when it wills to wander. As soon as we perceive that they have occurred, we drop them instantly and return to God, and thus, while the external senses of the spouse are asleep, the heart is watching; its love knows no intermission. A tender parent does not always bear his son distinctly in mind; he thinks and imagines a thousand things disconnected with him, but they do not interfere with the paternal affection. The moment that his thoughts rest again upon his child, he loves and feels in the depths of his soul that though he has ceased to think of him, he has not for an instant failed to love him. Such should be our love for our heavenly Father—simple, trustful, confident, and without anxiety.

If our imaginations take wings and our thoughts wander, let us not be perplexed; all these things are not that "*hidden man of the heart, in that which is not corruptible, even the ornament of a meek and quiet spirit*" (1 Peter 3:4), of which Saint Peter speaks. Let us only turn our thoughts, whenever we can, toward the face of the Well-Beloved without being troubled at our wanderings. When He shall see fit to enable us to preserve a more constant sense of His presence with us, He will do so.

He sometimes removes His presence for our advancement. It amuses us with too many reflections that are true distractions, diverting the mind from a simple and direct look toward God and withdrawing us from the shades of naked faith.

We often seek in these reflections a resting place for our self-love and consolation in the testimony we endeavor to extract from them for ourselves. Thus, the warmth of our feelings cause us to wander. On the contrary, we never pray so purely as when we are tempted to believe that we do not pray at all. We fear that we pray ill; but we should only fear being left to the desolation of sinful nature, to a philosophical infidelity that is perpetually seeking a demonstration of its own operations in faith—in short, to impatient desires for consolation in sight and feeling.

There is no more bitter penance than this state of pure faith without sensible support, and hence it seems to me the most effective, the most crucifying, and the least illusive. Strange temptation! We look impatiently for sensible consolation from the fear of not being penitent enough! Ah, why do we not consider the renouncement of that consolation that we are so strongly tempted to seek as a proof of our penitence? Remember that our Lord was abandoned by His Father on the cross. All feeling, all reflection was withdrawn, so that His God might be hidden from Him. This was indeed the last blow that fell upon the Man of Sorrows, the consummation of the sacrifice!

Never should we so abandon ourselves to God as when He seems to abandon us. Let us enjoy light and consolation when it is His pleasure to give it to us, but let us not attach ourselves to His gifts, but to Him. And when He plunges us into the night of pure faith, let us still press on through the agonizing darkness.

Moments are worth days in this tribulation. The soul is troubled and yet at peace; not only is God hidden from it, but it is hidden from itself so that *all* may be of faith. It is discouraged but feels, nevertheless, an immovable will to bear all that God may choose to inflict. It wills all and accepts all, even the troubles that try its faith, and thus in the very height of the tempest, the waters beneath are secretly calm and peaceful, because its will is one with God's. Blessed be the Lord who performs such great things in us, notwithstanding our unworthiness!

8

On Meditation

When the solid foundations of a perfect conversion of heart, a scrupulous repentance, and a serious meditation of all the Christian virtues have been established, both theoretically and practically, we become gradually so accustomed to these truths that we regard them at last with a simple and steady look, without the necessity of going back to examine and convince ourselves of each one of them in detail. They are then all embraced in a certain enjoyment of God, so pure and so intimate that we find everything in Him. It is no longer the intellect that examines and reasons; it is the will that loves and plunges into the infinite good.

But this is not your state. You must walk for a long while in the way of the sinners who are beginning to seek God; ordinary meditation is your lot, too happy that God condescends to admit you to it.

Walk then in the spirit, as Abraham, without knowing where you go; be content with your daily bread and remember that, in the desert, the manna of today cannot be preserved until tomorrow without its corruption. The children of God must be shut up to the grace of the present moment without desiring to foresee the designs of Providence concerning them.

Since now is your opportunity, meditate, then, upon all the mysteries of Jesus Christ and upon all the gospel truths that you have for so long a time ignored and rejected. When God will have entirely effaced from your mind the impression of all your worldly maxims, and the Spirit will have left there no trace of your old prejudices, then it will be necessary to ascertain the direction in which you are attracted by grace and to follow step-by-step, without anticipating.

In the meantime, dwell in peace in the bosom of God, as does a little child on the breast of his mother; be satisfied with thinking on your chosen subject simply and easily; suffer yourself to be led gently to the truths that affect you and that you find to nourish your heart. Avoid all exertions that excite the intellect, which often tempt us to believe that there is more piety in a dangerous vivacity of the imagination than in a pure and upright intention of abandonment to God. Avoid likewise all refined speculation; confine yourself to simple reflections and return to them frequently. Those who pass too rapidly from one truth to another feed their curiosity and restlessness; they even distract their intellect by too great a multiplicity of views.

Give every truth time to send down deep roots into the heart. The main point is to love. Nothing gives rise to such severe fits of indigestion as eating too much and too hastily. Digest every truth leisurely, if you would extract the essence of it for your nourishment; but let there be no restless, self-reflective acts. Be sure that your exercise will not be acceptable unless performed without agitation or tumult.

I am well aware that you will have distractions enough. Bear them without impatience; dismiss them and return quietly to your subject as soon as you perceive that your imagination has wandered. In this way, these involuntary distractions will produce no injurious effects, and the patience with which you bear them, without being discouraged, will advance you farther than a more continuous meditation, in which you might take more self-satisfaction. The true method of conquering wandering thoughts is never to attack them directly with bitterness, and never to be discouraged by their frequency or duration.

Allow yourself, then, to be quietly occupied by the subject you have chosen; only let the exercise be as holy as you can make it, to which end take the following directions:

Do not encumber yourself with a great number of thoughts upon a subject, but dwell upon each one sufficiently long enough to allow it to afford its proper nourishment to the heart. You will gradually become accustomed to regard each truth steadily by itself, without flitting from one to another. This habit will serve to fix them deeply in your soul. You will thus also acquire a habit of dwelling upon your themes with pleasure and peaceful acquiescence, instead of considering them rapidly and intellectually as most persons do. Thus, the foundations will be firmly laid for all that God intends to do in you; He will thus mortify the natural activity of the mind that ever inclines it to seek novelties instead of deeply imprinting the truths already in some degree familiar. You must not, however, forcibly restrain your mind to a subject that no longer seems to afford any nourishment. I would advise that you should not abandon it so long as it still ministers food.

As to your affections, retain all that the view of your subject naturally and quietly induces, but do not attempt to stir yourself up to great efforts, for they will exhaust and agitate you and even cause dryness; they will occupy you too much with your own exertions and implant a dangerous confidence on your own power. In short, they will attach you too firmly to sensible pleasures and will thus prepare for you great trouble. Be content, then, to follow with simplicity, and without too many reflections, the emotions that God will excite in view of your subject or of any other truth. As for higher things, have no thoughts of them; there is a time for everything, and it is of the greatest importance that nothing should be precipitated.

One of the cardinal rules of the spiritual life is that we are to live exclusively in the present moment without casting a look beyond. You remember that the Israelites in the desert followed the pillar of fire, or of cloud, without knowing where it was leading them. (See Exodus 13:21.) They had a supply of manna only for one day; all above that became useless. There is no necessity now for moving rapidly; think only of laying a solid foundation. See that it is deep and broad by an absolute renunciation of self and by abandonment without reserve to the requirements of God. Let God, then, raise upon this foundation such a building as He pleases. Shut your eyes and commit yourself to Him. How wonderful is this walking with Abraham in pure faith, not knowing where we go and how full of blessings the path is!

God will then be your guide; He Himself will travel with you, as we are told He did with the Israelites, to bring them step-by-step across the desert to the Promised Land. Ah, what will be your blessedness if you will but surrender yourself into the hands of God, permitting Him to do whatever He will, not according to your desires but according to His own good pleasure!

9

On Mortification

God calls us hourly and momentarily to the exercise of mortification, but nothing can be more false than the maxim that we should always choose that which mortifies us the most. Such a plan would soon destroy our health, our reputation, our business, our communion with our relatives and friends, and the good works that Providence requires of us. I have no hesitation in saying that we ought to avoid certain things that experience has shown to injure our health, such as certain kinds of food. This course will, no doubt, spare us some suffering, but it does not tend to pamper the body nor require the employment of expensive or delicious substitutes; on the contrary, it conduces to a sober, and, therefore, in many respects, mortified life.

Failures in regimen are owing to a want of mortification; they are not due to either courage in enduring pain or to indifference to life, but to a weak hankering for pleasure and a impatience for anything that annoys. Submitting to regimen for the purpose of preserving health is a great constraint; we would much rather suffer and be sick than be constantly restraining our appetites. We love liberty and pleasure more than health. But God arranges all of that in the heart that is devoted to Him; He causes us to fall in quietly with every regulation, and takes away a certain lack of pliability in the will and a dangerous confidence in ourselves. He blunts the desires, cools the passions, and detaches the man, not only from exterior things, but from himself; and He renders him mild, amiable, simple, lowly, and ready to will or not to will, according to His good pleasure. Let it be so with us. God desires it and is ready to do it. Let us not resist His will. The mortification that comes in the order of God is more serviceable than any enjoyment in devotion that would result from our own affection and choice.

In regard to austerities, everyone must regard his attraction, his state, his need, and his temperament. A simple mortification, consisting in nothing more than an unshaken fidelity in providential crosses, is often far more valuable than severe austerities that render the life more marked and tempt to a vain self-complacency. Whoever will refuse nothing that comes in the order of God and seek nothing out of that order need never fear to finish his day's work without partaking of the cross of Jesus Christ. There is an indispensable Providence for crosses as well as for the necessities of life; they are a part of our daily bread. God will never allow it to fail. It is sometimes a very useful mortification to certain fervent souls to give up their own plans of mortification and adopt with cheerfulness those that are momentarily revealed in the order of God.

When a soul is not faithful in providential mortifications, there is reason to fear some illusion in those that are sought through the fervor of devotion. Such warmth is often deceitful, and it seems to me that a soul in this case would do well to examine its faithfulness under the daily crosses allotted by Providence.

10

On Self-abandonment

If you would fully comprehend the meaning of self-abandonment,[1] recall the interior difficulty that you felt and that you very naturally testified when I directed you always to count as *nothing* this self that is so dear to us. To abandon oneself is to count oneself as nothing; and he who has perceived the difficulty of doing it has already learned what that renunciation is that so revolts our nature. Since you have felt the blow, it is evident that it has fallen upon the sore spot in your heart. Let the all-powerful hand of God work in you, as He well knows how, to tear you from yourself.

---

1. Note from the editor: The terms *abandonment, annihilation,* and *death,* of themselves, and the correlative expressions, *union with God, oneness,* and others of similar import, are frequently used by writers on the higher life as a most concise and convenient form of designating a state of experience indicated throughout the New Testament, by such texts as the following: "*Wherefore if ye be dead with Christ*" (Colossians 2:20); "*If ye then be risen with Christ*" (Colossians 3:1); "*For ye are dead, and your life is hid with Christ in God*" (Colossians 3:3); "*And they that are Christ's have crucified the flesh with the affections and lusts*" (Galatians 5:24); "*For it is God which worketh in you both to will and to do of his good pleasure*" (Philippians 2:13); and "*That they all may be one; as thou, Father, art in me, and I in thee, that they also may be one in us*" (John 17:21).

It has been objected by some, that this abnegation of self, recommended in such glowing terms by these pious authors, involved two exceedingly dangerous errors: That on the one hand, it necessarily implied an abandonment and loss of our identity, by a sort of pagan transfusion into God, and on the other, that it bordered upon, if it did not constitute, a very pernicious form of perfectionism, in that it made God the author of all our willing and doing whatever their moral character. It can scarcely be necessary to say to anyone who has made himself familiar with the subject that such doctrines would be a melancholy perversion of the teachings of the writers in question. By the death of self and the annihilation of the will simply mean

The origin of our trouble is that we love ourselves with a blind passion that amounts to idolatry. If we love anything beyond, it is only for our own sakes. We must be undeceived respecting all those generous friendships in which it appears as though we so far forgot ourselves as to think only of the interests of our friend. If the motive of our friendship be not low and gross, it is nevertheless still selfish, and the more delicate, the more concealed, and the more proper in the eyes of the world it is, the more dangerous it becomes and the more likely to poison us by feeding our self-love.

In those friendships that appear, both to ourselves and to the world, so generous and disinterested, we seek, in short, the pleasure of loving without recompense and, by the indulgence of so noble a sentiment, of raising ourselves above the weak and sordid of our race. Besides the tribute that we pay to our own pride, we seek from the world the reputation of disinterestedness and generosity; we desire to be loved by our friends, although we do not desire to be served by them. We hope that they will be charmed with what we do for them without any expectation of return, and in this way, we get that very return that we seem to despise. For what is more delicious to a delicate self-love than to hear itself applauded for not being self-love?

You may have seen someone who seemed to think of everyone but himself, who was the delight of good people, who was well disciplined, and who seemed entirely forgetful of self. The self-oblivion is so great that self-love even would imitate it and finds no glory equal to that of seeming to seek none at all. This moderation and self-renunciation that, if genuine, would be the death of nature, becomes

---

to express, in the strongest manner possible, that the soul, on every occasion, and under all circumstances, wills only what God wills, retaining perfectly its identity, and, of course, its power to will. By union with or absorption into God, they intend to convey the idea of the state of oneness referred to by Christ, wherein the soul is made partaker of the perfect holiness of God; but none are more earnest in insisting that the smallest appearance of evil is unanswerable evidence that such an attainment is still at a distance. "By their fruits you will know them" (see Matthew 7:16) is constantly asserted to be the inexorable standard of judgment for this, as for all other states of experience.

on the other hand the most subtle and imperceptible food of a pride that despises all ordinary forms of glory and desires only that which is to be secured by trampling under foot all the gross objects of ambition that captivate ordinary minds.

But it is not a difficult matter to unmask this modest arrogance—this pride that seems no pride at all, so much does it appear to have renounced all the ordinary objects of desire. Condemn it, and it cannot bear to be found at fault; let those whom it loves fail to repay it with friendship, esteem, and confidence, and it is stung to the quick. It is easy to see that it is not disinterested, though it tries so hard to seem so. It does not indeed accept payment in as gross coin as others; it does not desire insipid praise or money or that good fortune that consists in office and dignities. It must be paid, nevertheless; it is greedy of the esteem of good people; it loves that it may be loved again and be admired for its disinterestedness; it seems to forget self so that, by that means, it may draw the attention of the whole world upon self alone.

It does not, indeed, make all these reflections in full detail; it does not say in so many words, "I will deceive the whole world with my generosity in order that the world may love and admire me." No, it would not dare to address such a gross and unworthy language to itself; it *deceives* itself with the rest of the world; it admires itself in its generosity, as a belle admires her beauty in a mirror. It is affected by perceiving that it is more generous and more disinterested than the rest of mankind; the illusion it prepares for others extends to itself. It passes with itself for what it passes itself upon others, that is, for generosity, and this is what pleases it more than anything else.

However little we may have looked within ourselves to study the occasions of our pleasure and our grief, we will have no difficulty in admitting that pride, as it is more or less delicate, has various tastes. But give it what taste you will, it is still pride, and that which appears the most restrained and the most reasonable is the most devilish. In esteeming itself, it despises others; it pities those who are pleased with foolish vanities. It recognizes the emptiness of greatness and rank; it cannot abide those who are intoxicated with good fortune; it would, by its moderation, be above fortune, and thus it would raise itself to a new height by putting under foot all the false glory of men. Like Lucifer, it would become like the Most High. It would be a sort of divinity above all human passions and interests, not perceiving that it seeks to place itself above men by this deceitful pride that blinds it.

We may be sure, then, that it is the love of God only that can make us come out of self. If His powerful hand did not sustain us, we should not know how to take the first step in that direction.

There is no middle course; we must refer everything either to God or to self. If to self, we have no other God than self; if to God, we are then in order, and regarding ourselves only as one among the other creatures of God, without selfish interests and with a single *eye* to accomplish His will, we enter into the self-abandonment that we desire so earnestly to understand.

But let me say again that nothing will so shut your heart against the grace of abandonment as that philosophic pride and self-love in the disguise of worldly generosity, of which you should be especially in fear, on account of your natural disposition toward it. The greater our inherent endowment of frankness, disinterest, pleasure in doing good, delicacy of feeling, love of honor, and generous friendship, the more lively should be our distrust of self and our fear, lest we take complacency in these gifts of nature.

The reason why no creature can draw us out of ourselves is that there is none who deserves to be preferred before ourselves. There is none who has the right to detach us, nor the perfection that would be necessary to unite us to them without reference to ourselves, nor the power to satisfy the soul in such an attachment. Hence it is that we love nothing out of ourselves except for the reference it has to us.

We choose under the direction of our coarse and brutal passions if we are low and boorish, or under the guidance of a refined desire for glory if we are so delicate as not to be satisfied with what is gross and vulgar.

But God does two things that He only has the power to do. He reveals Himself to us, with all His rights over the creature and in all the charms of His goodness. Then we feel that, not having made ourselves, we are not made for ourselves—that we are created for the glory of Him who was pleased to form us, that He is too great to make anything except for Himself, and that all our perfection and happiness should be lost in Him.

This is what no created thing, dazzling though it may be, can make us realize in respect to ourselves. Far from finding in them that infinity that so fills and transports us in God, we discover only a void, a powerlessness to fill our hearts, an imperfection that continually drives us into ourselves.

The second miracle that God works is to operate in our hearts that which He pleases after having enlightened our understanding. He is not satisfied with having displayed his own charms; He makes us love Him by producing, by His grace, His love in our hearts, and He thus performs within us what He makes us see we owe to Him.

You desire, perhaps, to know in more detail in what this self-abandonment consists. I will endeavor to satisfy you.

There is little difficulty in comprehending that we must reject criminal pleasures, unjust gains, and gross vanities, because the renouncement of these things consists in a contempt that repudiates them absolutely and forbids us from deriving any enjoyment from them. But it is not so easy to understand that we must abandon property honestly acquired, the pleasures of a modest and well-spent life, the honors derivable from a good reputation, and a virtue that elevates us above the reach of envy.

The reason we do not understand that these things must be given up is that we are not required to discard them with dislike but, on the contrary, to preserve them to be used according to the station in which Divine Providence places us.

We have need of the consolation of a mild and peaceful life, to console us under its troubles; in respect to honors, we must regard "that which is convenient," and we must keep the property we possess to supply our wants. How then are we to renounce these things at the very moment when we are occupied in the care of preserving them? We are, moderately and without inordinate emotion, to do what is in our power to retain them, in order to make a sober use of them, without desiring to enjoy them or placing our hearts upon them.

I say a *sober use* of them because, when we are not attached to a thing for the purposes of self-enjoyment and of seeking our happiness in it, we use only so much of it as we are necessarily obliged to. As you may see, a wise and faithful steward studies to appropriate only so much of his master's property as is precisely requisite to meet his necessary wants.

The abandonment of evil things then consists in refusing them with horror; of good things, in using them with moderation for our necessities, continually studying to retrench all those imaginary wants with which greedy nature would flatter herself.

Remember that we must not only renounce evil but also good things, for Jesus has said, "*Whosoever he be of you that forsaketh not all he hath, he cannot be my disciple*" (Luke 14:33).

It follows, then, that the Christian must abandon everything he has, however innocent; for if he does not renounce it, it ceases to be innocent. He must abandon those things that it is his duty to guard with the greatest possible care, such as the good of his family, or his own reputation, for he must have his heart on none of these things. He must preserve them for a sober and moderate use; in short, he must be ready to give them all up whenever it is the will of Providence to deprive him of them. He must give up those whom he loves best and whom it is his duty to love; and his renouncement of them consists in this, that he is to love them for God only; to make use of the consolation of their friendship soberly, and for the supply of his wants; to be ready to part with them whenever God wills it; and to never seek in them the true repose of his heart. This is that chastity of true Christian friendship that seeks in the mortal and earthly friend only the heavenly spouse. It is thus that we use the world and the creature as not abusing them, according to Saint Paul. (See 1 Corinthians 7:31.) We do not desire to take pleasure in them; we use only what God gives us, what He wills that we should love, and what we accept with the reserve of a heart, receiving it for only necessity's sake, and keeping itself for a more worthy object.

It is in this sense that Christ would have us leave father and mother, brothers and sisters, and friends, and that He has come to bring a sword upon the earth. God is a jealous God; if, in the recesses of your soul, you are attached to any creature, your heart is not worthy of Him. He must reject this person as a spouse that divides her affections between her bridegroom and a stranger.

Having abandoned everything exterior, and that is not self, it remains to complete the sacrifice by renouncing everything interior, including self.

The renouncement of the body is frightful to most delicate and worldly minded persons. They know nothing, so to speak, that is more themselves than their body, which they flatter and adorn with so much care; and even when they are deprived of its graces, they often retain a love for it amounting to a shameful cowardice, so that the very name of death makes them shudder.

Your natural courage raises you above these fears, and I think I hear you say, I desire neither to flatter my body, nor to hesitate in consenting to its destruction, whenever it will be the will of God to waste and consume it to ashes.

You may thus renounce the body, and yet there may remain great obstacles in the way of your renouncing the spirit. The more we are able, by the aid of our natural courage, to despise the clay tenement, the more apt we are to set a higher value upon that which it contains, by the aid of which we are enabled to look down upon it.

We feel toward our understanding, our wisdom, and our virtue as a young and worldly woman feels toward her beauty. We take pleasure in them; it gives us a satisfaction to feel that we are wise, moderate, and preserved from the excitement that we see in others. We are intoxicated with the pleasure of not being intoxicated with pleasure. We renounce with courageous moderation the most flattering temptations of the world and content us with the satisfaction derived from a conviction of our self-control.

What a dangerous state! What a subtle poison! How recreant are you to God if you yield your heart to this refinement of self-love! You must renounce all satisfaction and all natural complacency in your own wisdom and virtue.

Remember, the purer and more excellent the gifts of God, the more jealous He is of them.

He showed mercy to the first human rebel and denied it to the angels. Both sinned by the love of self, but as the angel was perfect and regarded as a sort of divinity, God punished his unfaithfulness with a fiercer jealousy than He did man's disobedience. We may infer from this that God is more jealous of His most excellent gifts than He is of the more common ones. He would have us be attached to nothing but Himself, and regard His gifts, however excellent, as only the means of uniting us more easily and intimately to Him. Whoever contemplates the grace of God with a satisfaction and sort of pleasure of ownership turns it into poison.

Never appropriate exterior things to yourself, then, such as favor or talents or even the most interior things. Your good will is no less a gift of God's mercy than the life and being that you receive directly from His hands. Live, as it were, on trust; all that is in you and all that you are is only loaned you. Make use of it according to the will of Him who lends it, but never regard it for a moment as your own.

Herein consists true self-abandonment; it is this spirit of *self-divesting,* this use of ourselves and of ours with a single eye to the movements of God, who alone is the true proprietor of His creatures.

You will desire to know, probably, what should be the practice of this renouncement in detail. But I answer that the feeling is no sooner established in the interior of the soul than God Himself will take you by the hand, that you may be exercised in self-renunciation in every event of every day.

Self-abandonment is not accomplished by means of painful reflections and continual struggles; it is only by refraining from self-contemplation and by desiring to master ourselves in our own way that we lose ourselves in God.

11

On Temptations

I know of but two resources against temptations. One is faithfully to follow the interior light in sternly and immediately cutting off everything that we are at liberty to dismiss and that may excite or strengthen the temptation. I say *everything* that we are at liberty to dismiss, because we are not always permitted to avoid the occasions of evil. Such as are unavoidable, connected with the particular position in which Providence has placed us, and are not considered to be within our power.

The other expedient consists in turning toward God in every temptation, without being disturbed or anxious to know if we have not already yielded a sort of half consent, and without interrupting our immediate recourse to God. By examining too closely whether we have not been guilty of some unfaithfulness, we incur the risk of being again entangled in the temptation. The shortest and surest way is to act like a little child at the breast; when we show it a frightful monster, it shrinks back and buries its face in its mother's bosom so that it may no longer behold it.

The sovereign remedy is the habit of dwelling continually in the presence of God. He sustains us, consoles us, and calms us. We must never be astonished at temptations, be they never so outrageous. On this earth, all is temptation. Crosses tempt us by irritating our pride, and prosperity by flattering it. Our lives are a continual combat, but one in which Jesus Christ fights for us.

We must pass on unmoved while temptations rage around us, as the traveler, overtaken by a storm, simply wraps his cloak more closely about him and pushes on more vigorously toward his destined home.

If the thought of former sins and wretchedness should be permitted to come before us, we must remain confounded and abashed before God, quietly enduring in His adorable presence all the shame and ignominy of our transgressions. We must not, however, seek to entertain or to call up so dangerous a recollection.

In conclusion, it may be said that in doing what God wills, there is very little to be done by us, and yet there is a wonderful work to be accomplished, no less than that of reserving nothing and making no resistance for a moment to that jealous love that searches inexorably into the most secret recesses of the soul for the smallest trace of self, for the slightest intimations of an affection of which itself is not the author. So on the other hand, true progress does not consist in a multitude of views or in austerities, trouble, and strife. It is simply willing nothing and everything, without reservation and without choice, cheerfully performing each day's journey as Providence appoints it for us, seeking nothing, refusing nothing, finding everything in the present moment, and allowing God, who does everything, to do His pleasure in us and by us, without the slightest resistance. O how happy is he who has attained to this state! And how full of good things is his soul when it appears emptied of everything!

Let us ask the Lord to open to us the whole infinitude of His paternal heart, so that our own may be there submerged and lost, so that it may make but one with His! Such was the desire of Paul for the faithful, when he longed for them in the bowels of Jesus Christ.

12

On Wandering Thoughts and Dejection

Two things trouble you; one is how you may avoid wandering thoughts; the other, how you may be sustained against dejection. As to the former, you will never cure them by set reflections; you must not expect to do the work of grace by the resources and activity of nature. Be simply content to yield your will to God without reservation, and whenever any state of suffering is brought before you, accept it as His will in an absolute abandonment to His guidance.

Do not go out in search of these crucifixions, but when God permits them to reach you without you seeking them, they need never pass without your deriving profit from them.

Receive everything that God presents to your mind, notwithstanding the shrinking of nature, as a trial by which He would exercise and strengthen your faith. Never trouble yourself to inquire whether you will have strength to endure what is presented, if it should actually come upon you, for the moment of trial will have its appointed and sufficient grace; that of the present moment is to behold the afflictions presented tranquilly and to feel willing to receive them whenever it should be the will of God to bestow them.

Go on cheerfully and confidently in this trust. If this state of the will should not change in consequence of a voluntary attachment to something out of the will of God, it will continue forever.

Your imagination will doubtless wander to a thousand matters of vanity; it will be subject to more or less agitation according to your situation and the character of the objects presented to its regard. But what matter? The imagination, as Saint Theresa declares, is the fool of the household; it is constantly busy in making some bustle or other in order to distract the mind that cannot avoid beholding the images it exhibits. The attention is inevitable and is a true distraction, but so long as it is involuntary, it does not separate us from God; nothing can do that but some distraction of the will.

You will never have wandering thoughts if you never will to have them, and you may then say with truth that you have prayed without ceasing. Whenever you perceive that you have involuntarily strayed away, return without effort, and you will tranquilly find God again without any disturbance of soul. As long as you are not aware of it, it is no wandering of the heart; when it is made manifest, look to God at once with fidelity, and you will find that this simple faithfulness to Him will be the occasion of blessing you with His more constant and more familiar indwelling.

A frequent and easy recollection is one of the fruits of this faithful readiness to leave all wanderings as soon as they are perceived; but it must not be supposed that it can be accomplished by our own labors. Such efforts would produce trouble, scrupulosity, and restlessness in all those matters in which you have most occasion to be free. You will be constantly dreading lest you should lose the presence of God, and continually endeavoring to recover it. You will surround yourself with the creations of your own imagination. Thus, the presence of God, which will, by its sweetness and illumination, assist us in everything that comes before us in

His providence, will keep us always in a tumult and will render us incapable of performing the exterior duties of our condition.

Be never troubled, then, at the loss of the sensible presence of God, but above all, beware of seeking to retain Him by a multitude of argumentative and reflective acts. Be satisfied during the day and as you go about about the details of your daily duties, with a general and interior view of God, so that if asked, at any moment, whether your heart is tending, you may answer with truth that it is toward God, though the attention of your mind may then be engrossed by something else. Be not troubled by the wanderings of your imagination that you cannot restrain. How often do we wander through the fear of wandering and the regret that we have done so! What would you say of a traveler who, instead of constantly advancing on his journey, should employ his time in anticipating the falls that he might suffer or in weeping over the place where one had happened? "On, on!" you would say to him. "On, without looking behind or stopping." We must proceed as the apostle bids us to, so that we may abound more and more. (See 1 Thessalonians 4:1.) The abundance of the love of God will be of more service in correcting us than all our restlessness and selfish reflections.

This rule is simple enough, but nature, accustomed to the intricacies of reasoning and reflection, considers it as altogether too simple. We want to help ourselves and to communicate more impulse to our progress, but it is the very excellency of the precept that it confines us to a state of naked faith, sustained by God alone in our absolute abandonment to Him, and leads us to the death of self by stifling all remains of it whatsoever. In this way, we will not be led to increase the external devotional practices of such as are exceedingly occupied, or are feeble in body, but we will be contented with turning them all into simple love. Thus, we will only act as constrained by love and will never be overburdened, for we will only do what we love to do.

Dejection often arises from the fact that, in seeking God, we have not so found Him as to content us. The desire to find Him is not the desire to possess Him; it is simply a selfish anxiety to be assured, for our own consolation, that we do possess Him. Poor nature, depressed and discouraged, is impatient of the restraints of naked faith, where every support is withdrawn. It is grieved to be traveling, as it were, in the air, where it cannot behold its own progress toward perfection. Its pride is irritated by a view of its defects, and this sentiment is mistaken for humility. It longs, from self-love, to behold itself perfect; it is vexed that it is not so already. It is impatient, haughty, and out of temper with itself and everybody else. Sad state! As though the work of God could be accomplished by our ill-humor! As though the peace of God could be attained by means of such interior restlessness!

Martha, Martha, why are you troubled and anxious about so many things? One thing is needful, to love Him and to sit attentively at His feet! (See Luke 10:40–42.)

When we are truly abandoned to God, all things are accomplished without the performance of useless labor. We suffer ourselves to be guided in perfect trust. For the future, we will whatever God wills and shut our eyes to everything else; for the present, we give ourselves up to the fulfillment of His designs.

Sufficient for every day is the good and the evil of it. This daily doing of the will of God is the coming of His kingdom within us and, at the same time, our daily bread. We should be faithless indeed, and guilty of heathen distrust, if we desired to penetrate the future, which God has hidden from us. Leave it to Him; let Him make it short or long, bitter or sweet; let Him do with it even as it will please Him.

The most perfect preparation for this future, whatever it may be, is to die to every will of our own and yield ourselves wholly up to His will. We will, in this frame of mind, be ready to receive all the grace suitable to whatever state it shall be the will of God to develop in and around us.

When we are thus prepared for every event, we begin to feel the rock under our feet at the very bottom of the abyss. We are ready to suppose every imaginable evil of ourselves, but we throw ourselves blindly into the arms of God, forgetting and losing everything else. This forgetfulness of self is the most perfect renouncement of self and acceptance of God. It is the sacrifice of self-love. It would be a thousand times more agreeable to accuse and condemn ourselves, to torment our body and mind, rather than to forget.

Such abandonment is an annihilation of self-love, in which it no longer finds any nourishment. Then the heart begins to expand; we begin to feel lighter for having thrown off the burden of self, which we had formerly carried. We are astounded to behold the simplicity and straightness of the way. We thought there was a need of strife and constant exertion, but we now perceive that there is little to do; that it is sufficient to look to God with confidence, without reasoning either upon the past or the future, regarding Him as a loving Father who leads us every moment by the hand. If some distraction should hide Him for a moment, without stopping to look at it, we should simply turn again to Him from whom we had departed. If we commit faults, we repent with a repentance wholly of love; and as we return to God, He makes us feel whatever we ought to feel. Sin seems hideous, but we love the humiliation it causes, and for which God permitted it.

As the reflections of our pride upon our defects are bitter, disheartening, and vexatious, so the return of the soul toward God is recollected, peaceful, and sustained by confidence. You will find by experience how much more your progress will be aided by this simple, peaceful turning to God than by all your chagrin and spite at the faults that exist in you. Only be faithful in turning quietly toward God alone the moment you perceive what you have done. Do not stop to argue with yourself; you can gain nothing from that quarter. When you accuse yourself of your misery, I see only you and yourself in consultation, poor wisdom that will issue from where God is not!

Whose hand is it that must pluck you out of the mire? Your own? Alas, you are buried deeper than thought and cannot help yourself; and more, this very slough is nothing but self. The whole of your trouble consists in the inability to leave yourself. Do you expect to increase your chances by dwelling constantly upon your defects and feeding your sensitiveness by a view of your folly? You will, in this way, only increase your difficulties, while the gentlest look toward God would calm your heart. It is His presence that causes us to go forth from self; and when He has accomplished that, we are in peace. But how are we to go forth? Simply by turning gently toward God and gradually forming the habit of so doing, by a faithful persistence in it, whenever we perceive that we have wandered from Him.

As to that natural dejection that arises from a melancholic temperament, it belongs purely to the body and is the province of the physician. It is true that it is constantly recurring, but let it be borne in peace, as we receive from His hands a fever or any other bodily ailment.

The question is not what is the state of our feelings but what is the condition of our will. Let us will to have what is the condition of our will. Let us will to have whatever we have and not to have whatever we have not. We would not even be delivered from our sufferings, for it is God's place to apportion to us our crosses and our joys. In the midst of affliction, we rejoice, as did the apostle, but it is not joy of the feelings but of the will. The wicked are wretched in the midst of their pleasures, because they are never content with their state; they are always desiring to remove some thorn or to add some flower to their present condition. The faithful soul, on the other hand, has a will that is perfectly free; it accepts, without questioning, whatever bitter blessings God develops, and wills them, loves them, and embraces them. It would not be freed from them, if it could be accomplished by a simple wish; for such a wish would be an act originating in self, and contrary to its abandonment to Providence, desiring that this abandonment should be absolutely perfect.

If there is anything capable of setting a soul in a large place, it is this absolute abandonment to God. It diffuses in the soul a peace that flows as a river and a righteousness that is as the waves of the sea. (See Isaiah 48:18.) If there is anything that can render the soul calm, dissipate its scruples, dispel its fears, sweeten its sufferings by the anointing of love, impart strength to it in all its actions, and spread abroad the joy of the Holy Spirit in its countenance and words, it is this simple, free, and childlike repose in the arms of God.

13

On Confidence in God

The best rule we can ever adopt is to receive equally and with the same submission everything that God sends us during the day, both within and without.

Without, there are things disagreeable that must be met with courage and things pleasant that must not be suffered to arrest our affections. We resist the temptations of the former by accepting them at once, and of the latter by refusing to admit them into our hearts. The same curse is necessary in regard to the interior life; whatever is bitter serves to crucify us and works all its benefit in the soul if we receive it simply, with a willingness that knows no bounds and a readiness that seeks no alleviation.

Pleasant gifts, which are intended to support our weakness by giving us a sensible consolation in our external acts, must be accepted with equal satisfaction, but in a different way. They must be received because God sends them, not because they are agreeable to our own feelings. They are to be used, like any other medicine, without self-complacency, without attachment to them, and without appropriation. We must accept them, but not hold on to them, so that when God sees fit to withdraw them, we may neither be dejected nor discouraged.

The source presumption lies in attachment to these transitory and sensible gifts. We imagine we have no regard to anything but the gift of God, while we are really looking to self, appropriating

His mercy and mistaking it for Him. And thus we become discouraged whenever we find that we have been deceived in ourselves. The soul that is sustained upon God, however, is not surprised at its own misery; it is delighted to find new proof that it can do nothing of itself and that God must do everything. I am never in the least troubled at being poor when I know that my Father has infinite treasures that He will give me. We will soon become independent of trust in ourselves if we suffer our hearts to feed upon absolute confidence in God.

We must count less upon sensible delights, and the measures of wisdom that devise for our own perfection, than upon simplicity, lowliness, renunciation of our own efforts, and perfect pliability to all the designs of grace. Everything else tends to emblazon our virtues and thus inspire a secret reliance upon our own resources.

Let us pray to God that He would root out of our hearts everything of our own planting and set out there, with His own hands, the Tree of Life, bearing all manner of fruits.

14

On What Manner We Are to Watch Ourselves

The following seem to me to be useful practical directions as to the manner in which we ought to watch ourselves without being too much occupied with the duty.

The wise and diligent traveler watches all his steps and keeps his eyes always directed to that part of the road that is immediately before him; he does not incessantly look backward to count his steps and examine his footmarks. He would lose time and hinder his progress by so doing.

The soul that God truly leads by the hand (for I do not now speak of those who are learning to walk and who are yet looking for the road) ought to watch its path, but with a simple, tranquil vigilance confined to the present moment, and without restlessness from love of self. Its attention should be continually directed to the will of God, in order to fulfill it every instant and not be engaged in reflex acts upon itself to be assured of its state, when God prefers it should be uncertain. Thus the psalmist exclaims, *"Mine eyes are ever toward the Lord; for he shall pluck my feet out of the net"* (Psalm 25:15).

Observe how, in order to keep his feet in safety in a way sown with snares, he raises his eyes to the Lord instead of fixing them upon the ground to scrutinize every step. We never watch so diligently over ourselves as when we walk in the presence of God, as

He commanded Abraham to do. In fact, what should be the end of all our vigilance? To follow step-by-step the will of God. He who conforms to that in all things watches over himself and sanctifies himself in everything.

If, then, we never lost sight of the presence of God, we should never cease to watch, and always with a simple, lovely, quiet, and disinterested vigilance. While on the other hand, the watchfulness that is the result of a desire to be assured of our state is harsh, restless, and full of self. We must not walk by our own light but by that of God. We cannot behold the holiness of God without feeling horror at the smallest of our transgressions.

In addition to the presence of God and a state of recollection, we may add the examination of conscience according to our need but conducted in a way that grows more and more simple, easy, and destitute of restless self-contemplations. We examine ourselves not for our own satisfaction but to conform to the advice we receive, and to accomplish the will of God.

In short, we abandon ourselves into the hands of God, and are just as happy in knowing ourselves there, as we should be miserable if we were in our own. We desire to see nothing of what it pleases Him to conceal. As we love Him infinitely more than we do ourselves, we make an unconditional sacrifice of ourselves to His good pleasure, desiring only to love Him and to forget ourselves. He who thus generously loses his soul will find it again with eternal life.

15

On the Inward Teaching of the Spirit of God

It is certain from the Holy Scriptures that the Spirit of God dwells and acts within us; prays without ceasing; groans, desires, and asks for us what we know not how to ask for ourselves; urges us on; animates us; speaks to us when we are silent; suggests to us all truth; and so unites us to Him that we become one spirit. (See John 14; Romans 8; 1 Corinthians 6:17.) This is the teaching of faith, and even those instructors who are farthest removed from the interior life cannot avoid acknowledging so much. Still, notwithstanding these theoretical principles, they always strive to maintain that in practice the external law, or at least a certain light of learning and reason, illuminates us within, and that then our understanding acts of itself from that instruction. They do not rely sufficiently upon the interior teacher, the Holy Spirit, who does everything in us. He is the soul of our soul; we could not form a thought or a desire without Him. Alas, what blindness is ours! We reckon ourselves alone in the interior sanctuary when God is much more intimately present there than we are ourselves.

"What, then?" you will say. "Are we all inspired?" Yes, doubtless, but not as were the prophets and apostles. Without the actual inspiration of the Spirit of grace, we could not do, will, or believe any good thing. We are, then, always inspired, but we incessantly stifle the inspiration. God does not cease to speak, but the noise of the creatures without and of our passions within confines us and prevents our hearing. We must silence every creature, including self, that in the deep stillness of the soul, we may perceive the ineffable voice of the Bridegroom. We must lend an attentive ear, for His voice is soft and still and is only heard by those who hear nothing else!

Ah, how rare is it to find a soul still enough to hear God speak! The slightest murmur of our vain desires or of a love fixed upon self confounds all the words of the Spirit of God. We hear well enough that He is speaking and that He is asking for something, but we cannot distinguish what is said and are often glad enough that we cannot. The least reserve, the slightest self-reflective act, the most imperceptible fear of hearing too clearly what God demands, interferes with the interior voice. Need we be astonished, then, if so many people, pious indeed, but full of amusements, vain desires, false wisdom, and confidence in their own virtues, cannot hear it and consider its existence as a dream of fanatics? Alas! what would they with their proud reasoning? Of what efficacy would be the exterior word of pastors, or even of the Scriptures themselves, if we had not within the word of the Holy Spirit giving to the others all their vitality? The outward word, even of the gospel, without the fecundating, vivifying, interior word, would be but an empty sound. It is the *letter* that alone kills, and the *Spirit* alone can give us life. (See 2 Corinthians 3:6.)

O eternal and omnipotent word of the Father, it is You who speaks in the depth of our souls! The word that proceeded from the mouth of the Savior, during the days of His mortal life, has only had energy to produce such wondrous fruits because it has been animated by that Spirit of life who is the Word Himself. Hence it is that Saint Peter says, *"Lord, to whom shall we go? Thou hast the words of eternal life"* (John 6:68).

It is not, then, the outward law of the gospel alone that God shows us internally, by the light of reason and faith; it is His Spirit that speaks, touches, operates in, and animates us. So it is the Spirit that does in us and with us whatever we do that is good, as it is our soul that gives life to our bodies and regulates all its movements.

It is, then, true that we are continually inspired and that we do not lead a gracious life, except insofar as we act under this interior inspiration. But O God, how few Christians feel it! How few are those who do not annihilate it by their voluntary distractions or by their resistance!

Let us recognize, then, the fact that God is incessantly speaking in us.[2] He speaks in the impenitent also, but, stunned by the noise of the world and their passions, they cannot hear Him; the interior voice is to them a fable. He speaks in awakened sinners; they are sensible of remorse of conscience, which is the voice of God reproaching them inwardly for their sins. When they are deeply moved, they have no difficulty in understanding about this interior voice, for it is it that pierces them so sharply. It is in them that the two-edged sword, of which Paul speaks, is "*piercing even to the dividing asunder of soul and spirit*" (Hebrews 4:12). God causes Himself to be perceived, enjoyed, and followed; they hear that sweet voice that buries a reproach in the bottom of the heart and causes it to be torn in pieces. Such is true and pure contrition.

God speaks, too, in wise and enlightened persons whose lives, outwardly correct, seem adorned with many virtues; but such are often too full of themselves and their lights to listen to God. Everything is turned into reasoning; they substitute the principles of natural wisdom and the plans of human prudence for what would come infinitely better through the channel of simplicity and docility to the Word of God. They seem good, sometimes better than

2. See Thomas à Kempis, *Of the Imitation of Christ* (New Kensington, PA: Whitaker House, 1981), 88.

others; they are so, perhaps, up to a certain point, but it is a mixed goodness. They are still in possession of themselves and desire always to be so, according to the measure of their reason; they love to be in the hands of their own counsel and to be strong and great in their own eyes.

I thank You, O my God, with Jesus Christ, that You have hidden Your ineffable secrets from these great and wise ones, while You take pleasure in revealing them to feeble and humble souls! It is with babes alone that You are wholly unreserved; You treat the others in their own way. They desire knowledge and great virtues, and You give them dazzling illuminations and convert them into heroes. But this is not the better part; there is something more hidden for Your dearest children. They lie with John on Your breast. As for these great ones who are constantly afraid of stooping and becoming lowly, You leave them in all their greatness; they will never share Your caresses and Your familiarity, for to deserve these, they must become as little children and play upon Your knees. (See Matthew 18:3.)

I have often observed that a rude, ignorant sinner, just beginning to be touched by a lively sense of the love of God, is much more disposed to listen to this inward language of the Spirit of grace than those enlightened and learned persons who have grown old in their own wisdom. God, whose sole desire is to communicate Himself, cannot, so to speak, find where to set His foot in souls so full of themselves, who have grown fat upon their own wisdom and virtues. But Scripture says, "*His secret is with the righteous*" (Proverbs 3:32).

But where are they? I do not find them. God sees them and loves to dwell in them. "*My Father will love him,*" says Jesus Christ, "*and we will come unto him, and make our abode with him*" (John 14:23). Ah! A soul delivered from self and abandoned to grace, counting itself as nothing, and walking, without thought, at the will of that pure love that is its perfect guide, has an experience that the wise can neither receive nor understand!

I was once as wise as any; thinking I saw everything; but I saw nothing. I crept along feeling my way by a succession of reasonings, but there was no ray to enlighten my darkness. I was content to reason. But when we have silenced everything within, that we may listen to God, we know all things without knowing anything, and then perceive that, until then, we were utterly ignorant of all that we had thought we understood. We lose all that we once had and care not for it. We have then no more that belongs to self; all things are lost, and we with them. There is something within us that joins with the spouse in Song of Solomon, saying, *"Let me see thy countenance, let me hear thy voice; for sweet is thy voice, and thy countenance is comely"* (Song of Solomon 2:14). Ah! How sweet is that voice. It makes me all tremulous within! Speak, O Beloved, and let none other dare to speak but You! Be still, my soul; speak, Love!

Then it is that we know all things without knowing anything. Not that we have the presumption to suppose that we possess in ourselves all truth. No! On the contrary, we feel that we see nothing, can do nothing, and are nothing; we feel it and are delighted at it. But in this unreserved abandonment, we find everything we need from moment to moment in the infinity of God. There we find the daily bread of knowledge, as of everything else, without lying up; then the unction from above teaches us all truth, while it takes away our own wisdom, glory, interest, and even our own will. It makes us content with our powerlessness and with a position below every creature; we are ready to yield to the merest worms of the dust and to confess our most secret miseries before the whole world, fearing unfaithfulness more than punishment and confusion of face.

Here it is, I say, that the Spirit teaches us all truth, for all truth is eminently contained in this sacrifice of love, where the soul strips itself of everything to present it to God.

16

On Daily Faults and the Toleration of Ourselves

You understand that many of our faults are voluntary in different degrees, though they may not be committed with a deliberate purpose of failing in our allegiance to God. One friend sometimes reproaches another for a fault not expressly intended to be offensive, and yet committed with the knowledge that it would be so. In the same way, God lays these sorts of faults to our charge. They are voluntary, for although not done with an express intention, they are still committed freely and against a certain interior light of conscience, which should have caused us to hesitate and wait.

Of these offenses, pious souls are often guilty; as to those of deliberate purpose, it would be strange indeed if a soul consecrated to God should fall into such.

Little faults become great and even monstrous in our eyes in proportion to the extent that the pure light of God increases in us, just as the sun in rising reveals the true dimensions of objects that were dimly and confusedly discovered during the night. Be sure that, with the increase of the inward light, the imperfections that you have, up to this point, seen will be beheld as far greater and more deadly in their foundations than you now conceive them, and that you will witness, in addition, the development of a crowd of others, of the existence of which you have not now the slightest suspicion. You will there find the weaknesses necessary to deprive you of all confidence in your own strength. But this discovery, far from discouraging, will serve to destroy your self-reliance and to raze to the ground the edifice of pride. Nothing marks so decidedly the solid progress of a soul as its ability to view its own depravity without being disturbed or discouraged.

It is an important precept to abstain from doing a wrong thing whenever we perceive it in time and, when we do not, to bear the humiliation of the fault courageously. If a fault is perceived before it is committed, we must see to it that we do not resist and quench the Spirit of God who is advising us of it inwardly. The Spirit is easily offended and very jealous; He desires to be listened to and obeyed. He retires if He is displeased. The slightest resistance to Him is a wrong, for everything must yield to Him the moment He is perceived. Faults of haste and frailty are nothing in comparison with those where we shut our ears to the voice of the Holy Spirit beginning to speak in the depths of the heart.

Restlessness and an injured self-love will never mend those faults that are not perceived until after they are committed; on the contrary, such feelings are simply the impatience of wounded pride at beholding what confounds it. We must quietly humble ourselves in peace; I say in *peace,* for it is no humiliation to do it in a vexed and spiteful way. We must condemn our faults, mourn over them, and repent of them, without seeking the slightest shadow of consolation in any excuse; and we must behold ourselves covered with confusion in the presence of God. All this we must do without being bitter against ourselves or discouraged, but peacefully reaping the profit of our humiliation. Thus from the Serpent himself, we draw the antidote to his venom.

It often happens that what we offer to God is not what He most desires to have of us; He wants what we are frequently the most unwilling to give, and of the most fearful He will ask. He desires sacrifices like Abraham's offering of Isaac, the well-beloved son; all the rest is as nothing in His eyes, and He permits it to be offered in a painful unprofitable manner, because He has no blessings for a divided soul. He will have everything, and until then, there is no rest. *"Who hath hardened himself against him, and hath prospered?"* (Job 9:4). Would you prosper and secure the blessing of God upon your labors? Reserve nothing, cut to the quick and burn, spare nothing, and the God of peace will be with you. What consolation, what liberty, what strength, what enlargement of heart, what increase of grace will follow when there remains nothing between God and the soul, and when the last sacrifices have been offered up without hesitation!

We must neither be astonished nor disheartened. We are not more wicked than we were; we are really less so, but while our evil diminishes, our light increases, and we are struck with horror at its extent. But let us remember, for our consolation, that the perception of our disease is the first step to the cure. When we have no sense of our need, we have no curative principle within; it is a state of blindness, presumption, and insensibility in which we are delivered over to our own counsel and commit ourselves to the current, fatal rapidity of which we do not realize until we are called to struggle against it.

We must not be discouraged either by experience of our weakness or by dislike of the constant activity that may be inseparable from our condition in life. Discouragement is not a fruit of humility but of pride; nothing can be worse. Suppose we have stumbled or even fallen; let us rise and run again. All our falls are useful if they strip us of a disastrous confidence in ourselves, and do not take away a humble and salutary trust in God.

The repugnance we feel toward our duties comes, no doubt, from imperfections; if we were perfect, we should love everything in the order of God, but since we are born corrupt and with a nature revolting against His laws, let us praise Him that He knows how to evolve good from evil and can make use of even our repugnance as a source of virtue. The work of grace does not always advance as regularly as that of nature, says Saint Teresa.

Carefully purify your conscience, then, from daily faults; suffer no sin to dwell in your heart. Small as it may seem, it obscures the light of grace, weighs down the soul, and hinders that constant communion with Jesus Christ, which should be your pleasure to cultivate. You will become lukewarm, forget God, and find yourself growing in attachment to the creature. A pure soul, on the other hand, which is humiliated, and rises promptly after its smallest faults, is always fervent and always upright.

God never makes us sensible of our weakness except to give us His strength. We must not be disturbed by what is involuntary. The great point is never to act in opposition to the inward light and to be willing to go as far as God would have us go.

17

On Fidelity in Small Matters

Saint Francis of Sales says that great virtues and fidelity in small things are like sugar and salt; sugar is more delicious but of less frequent use, while salt enters into every article of our food. Great virtues are rare; they are seldom needed, and when the occasion comes, we are prepared for it by everything that has preceded it, excited by the greatness of the sacrifice, and sustained either by the brilliancy of the action in the eyes of others or by self-complacency in our ability to do such wonderful things. Small occasions, however, are unforeseen; they recur every moment and place us incessantly in conflict with our pride, our sloth, our self-esteem, and our passions. They are calculated thoroughly to subdue our wills, and leave us no retreat. If we are faithful in them, nature will have no time to breathe and must die to all her inclinations. It would please us much better to make some great sacrifices, however painful and violent, on condition of obtaining liberty to follow our own pleasure, and retain our old habits in little things. But it is only by this fidelity in small matters that the grace of true love is sustained and distinguished from the transitory excitements of nature.

It is with piety as it is with our temporal goods; there is more danger from little expenses than from larger disbursements, and he who understands how to take care of what is insignificant will soon accumulate a large fortune. Everything great owes its greatness to the small elements of which it is composed. He who loses nothing will soon be rich.

Consider, on the other hand, that God does not regard our actions as much as the motive of love from which they spring and the pliability of our wills to His. Men judge our deeds by their outward appearance; God does not take account of that which is most dazzling in the eyes of man. What He desires is a pure intention, a will ready for anything and ever pliable in His hands, and an honest abandonment of self. All this can be much more frequently manifested in small, rather than extraordinary, occasions. There will also be much less danger from pride, and the trial will be far more searching. Indeed, it sometimes happens that we find it harder to part with a trifle than with an important interest; it may be more of a cross to abandon a vain amusement than to bestow a large sum in charity.

We are the more easily deceived about these small matters to the degree that we imagine them to be innocent and ourselves indifferent to them. Nevertheless, when God takes them away, we may easily recognize, in the pain of the deprivation, how excessive and inexcusable were both our use of them and our attachment to them. If we are in the habit of neglecting little things, we will be constantly offending our families, our domestics, and the public. No one can well believe that our piety is sincere when our behavior is loose and irregular in its little details. What ground do we have for believing that we are ready to make the greatest sacrifices when we daily fail in offering the least?

But the greatest danger of all consists in this: by neglecting small matters, the soul becomes accustomed to unfaithfulness. We grieve the Holy Spirit, we return to ourselves, and we think it a little thing to be wanting toward God. On the other hand, true love can see nothing small; everything that can either please or displease God seems to be great. Not that true love disturbs the soul with scruples, but it puts no limits to its faithfulness. It acts simply with God, and as it does not concern itself about those things that God does not require from it, so it never hesitates an instant about those that He does require, be they great or small.

Thus it is not by incessant care that we become faithful and exact in the smallest things, but simply by a love that is free from the reflections and fears of restless and scrupulous souls. We are, as it were, drawn along by the love of God; we have no desire to do anything but what we do, and no will in respect to anything that we do not do. At the very moment when God is following the soul, relentlessly pursuing it into the smallest details, and seemingly depriving it of all its liberty, it finds itself in a large place and enjoys a perfect peace in Him. Happy soul!

Those persons who are by nature less strict in small matters should lie down and preserve inviolate the most rigid laws in respect to them. They are tempted to despise them; they habitually think little of them and do not sufficiently estimate their importance. They do not consider the insensible progress of their passions and even forget their own sad experience on the subject. They prefer rather to be deluded by the promise of an imaginary firmness and to trust in their own courage, which has so often deceived them, than to subject themselves to a never-ceasing fidelity. "It is a small matter," say they; true, but it is of amazing consequence to you. It is a matter that you love well enough to refuse to give it up to God, a matter that you sneer at in words so that you may have a pretence to retain it. It is a small matter, but one that you withhold from your Maker, and which will prove your ruin.

It is no nobility of soul that despises small things; on the contrary, it is a contracted spirit that regards as unimportant what it cannot trace to its necessary and overwhelming results. The more trouble it occasions us to be on our guard against small matters, the more need have we to fear negligence, to distrust our strength, and to interpose impregnable barriers between ourselves and the least remissness.

Finally, judge by your own feelings. What would you think of a friend who owed everything to you and who was willing, from a sense of duty, to serve you on those rare occasions that are called great, but who should manifest neither affection nor the least regard for your wishes in the common intercourse of life?

Do not be frightened at this minute attention to small matters. It needs courage at first, but this is a penance that you deserve, that you need, and that will work out for you peace and security. Without it, all is trouble and relapse. God will gradually make it pleasant and easy to you, for true love is obedient without constraint and without strife or effort.

18

On Transitory Emotions, Fidelity, and Simplicity

We must not be surprised if we frequently perceive in ourselves emotions of pride, self-complacency, self-confidence, desires to follow our own inclination contrary to what is right, and impatience at the weakness of others, or the annoyances of our own state. In such cases, we must instantly let them drop like a stone to the bottom of the sea, recollect ourselves in God, and wait before acting until we are in such a frame of mind as our recollection should induce in us. If the distraction of business or of vivacity of imagination should hinder us from calmly and easily entering into such a state, we must at least endeavor to be quiet by the rectitude of the will and by the desire for recollection. In such a case, the will to be recollected answers to deprive the soul of its own will and to render it docile in the hands of God.

If perchance in your excitement, some emotion too nearly allied to depraved nature should have escaped you, be not discouraged; go straight on. Quietly bear the humiliation of your fault before God without being delayed by the smarting of self-love at the betrayal of its weakness. Proceed confidently without being troubled by the anguish of a wounded pride, which cannot bear to see itself imperfect. Your fault will be of service in causing you to die to self and to become nothing before Him.

The true method of curing this defect is to become dead to the sensitiveness of self-love, without hindering the course of grace, which has been a little interrupted by this transitory unfaithfulness.

The great point is to renounce your own wisdom by simplicity of walk, and to be ready to give up the favor, esteem, and approbation of every one, whenever the path in which God leads you passes that way. We are not to meddle with things that God does not lay upon us, or uselessly utter hard sayings that those around us are not able to bear.

We must follow after God, never precede Him; when He gives the signal, we must leave all and follow Him. If, after an absolute consecration to Him, and a conviction in conscience that He requires something of us, we hesitate, delay, lose courage, dilute what He would have us do, indulge fears for our own comfort or safety, desire to shield ourselves from suffering and obloquy, or seek to find some excuse for not performing a difficult and painful duty, we are truly guilty in His sight. God keep you from such unfaithfulness! Nothing is more dreadful than this inward resistance to Him; it is that sin against the Holy Ghost of which our Lord assures us *"shall not be forgiven...neither in this world, neither in the world to come"* (Matthew 12:32).

Other faults committed in the simplicity of your good intentions will be of service if they produce humility and render you of less account in your own eyes. But resistance to the Spirit of God through pride and a pusillanimous worldly wisdom, tender of its own comfort in performing the work of God, is a fault that will insensibly quench the Spirit of grace in your heart. God, jealous and rejected after so much mercy, will depart and leave you to your own resources. You will then turn around in a kind of circle instead of advancing with rapid strides along the King's highway.

Your inward life will grow dimmer and dimmer, without you being able to detect the sure and deep-seated source of your disease.

God would behold in you a simplicity that will contain so much the more of His wisdom as it contains less of your own. He desires to see you lowly in your own eyes and as docile as a babe in His hands. He desires to create in your heart that childlike disposition so distasteful to the spirit of man, but so agreeable to the Spirit of the gospel, in spite of the infection of a scornful and contemptuous world.

By this very simplicity and lowliness, He will heal all the remains of haughty and self-confident wisdom in you, and you will say with David, "*And I will yet be more vile than thus, and will be base in mine own sight*" (2 Samuel 6:22), from the moment that you give yourself to the Lord.

19

On the Advantages of Silence and Recollection

You must endeavor to be as silent as the proprieties of human communion will permit. This grace cherishes the presence of God, saves us many proud and rude expressions, and suppresses a great multitude of idle words and dangerous judgments of our neighbor. Silence humbles our spirit and gradually detaches it from the world; it constitutes in the heart a sort of solitude as that which you so much long after, and it will supply all your wants in the many perplexities that surround you. If we never unnecessarily open our mouths, we may enjoy many moments of communion even when unavoidably detained in society.

You desire to be at liberty so that you may pray to God; and God, who knows so much better what you want than you do, sends perplexity and restraint so that you may become mortified. This trial from the hand of God will be far more serviceable to you than the self-sought sweetness of prayer. You know very well that constant retirement is not necessary in order to love God. When He gives you the time, take it and profit by it, but until then, wait in faith, well persuaded that what He orders is best.

Frequently raise your heart to Him in abstraction from the world; speak only when obliged to; bear with patience whatever happens to cross you. You are already acquainted with religion, and God treats you according to your necessity. You have more need of mortification than of illumination. The only thing I fear for you in this state is wanderings; but you may avoid those by silence. Only be faithful in keeping silent when it is not necessary to speak, and God will send grace to preserve you from dissipation when it is.

When you are not permitted to enjoy long seasons of leisure, economize the short ones; ten minutes thus faithfully employed before God, in the midst of your distractions, will be as valuable to you as whole hours devoted to Him in your more unoccupied moments. Further, these little odds and ends of time will amount to quite a sum in the course of the day, and present this advantage—that God will very likely have been more in mind than if you had given it to Him all at once. Love, silence, suffering, yielding our own pleasure to the will of God, and loving our neighbor—such is our portion; we are too happy in bearing the burden that God Himself lays upon us in the order of His providence!

The crosses that originate with us are not near as efficient in eradicating self-love as those that come in daily allotments from God. The latter contribute no ailment for the nourishment of our own wills, and as they proceed immediately from a merciful Providence, they are accompanied by grace sufficient for all our needs. We have nothing to do, then, but to surrender ourselves to God each day, without looking further. He will carry us in His arms as a tender mother bears her child. Let us believe, hope, and love with all the simplicity of babes; in every necessity, turning a loving and trusting look toward our heavenly Father. For Scripture says, "*Can a woman forget her sucking child, that she should not have compassion on the son of her womb? Yea, they may forget, yet will I not forget thee*" (Isaiah 49:15).

20

On Privation and Annihilation—Terrors to the Spiritually Minded

There is scarce anyone who desires to serve God, but does so for selfish reasons. We expect gain and not loss, consolation and not suffering, riches and not poverty, increase and not diminution. But the whole interior work is of an opposite character—to be lost, sacrificed, made less than nothing, and despoiled of an excessive delight, even in the gifts of God, so that we may be forced to cling to Him alone.

We are as a patient who, in eagerly desiring to return to health, feels his own pulse forty times a day, and requires his physician to prescribe frequent doses of various remedies, as well as a daily assurance that he is getting better. Such is almost the only use we make of our spiritual conductors. We travel in a little round of everyday virtues, never gathering sufficient courage to pass generously beyond it, and our guides, like the doctor, flatter, console, encourage, and strengthen our selfish sensitiveness and administer pleasant remedies, to the effects of which we soon become insensible.

The moment we find ourselves deprived of the delights of grace, that milk for babes, we are at once in despair—a manifest proof that we were looking to the means, instead of to the end, and solely for selfish gratification.

Privations are meat for men; by them the soul is rendered hardy, is separated from self, and is offered in a pure sacrifice to God. But we give up all the moment they commence. We cannot but think that everything is going to ruin when, in fact, the foundations are just beginning to be solidly laid. Nothing would give us more delight than God doing all to His pleasure with us, provided it should always be to magnify and perfect us in our own eyes. But if we are not willing to be destroyed and annihilated, we will never become that whole "burnt offering" that is entirely consumed in the blaze of God's love.

We desire to enter into a state of pure faith and to retain our own wisdom! To be a babe and great in our own eyes! Ah, what a sad delusion!

21

On the Proper Use of Crosses

We are hardly to be persuaded of the goodness of God in loading those whom He loves with crosses. Why, we say, should He take pleasure in causing us to suffer? Could He not render us good without making us miserable? Yes, doubtless, He could, for all things are possible with God. He holds in His omnipotent hands the hearts of men, and turns them as He will, as the skill of the workman can give direction to the stream on the summit of a hill. But able as He was to save us without crosses, He has not chosen to do it, as He has not seen fit to create men at once in the full vigor of manhood, but has allowed them to grow up by degrees amid all the perils and weaknesses of infancy and youth. In this matter, He is the Master; we have only to adore in silence the depths of His wisdom without comprehending it. Nevertheless, we see clearly that we never could become wholly good without becoming humble, unselfish, and disposed to refer everything to God without any restless, self-reflective acts.

The work of grace, in detaching us from self and destroying our self-love, could not be anything other than painful without a miracle. Neither in His gracious nor providential dealings does God work a miracle lightly. It would be as great a wonder to see a person full of self become in a moment dead to all self-interest and all sensitiveness as it would be to see a slumbering infant wake in the morning a fully developed man. God works in a mysterious way in grace as well as in nature, concealing His operations under an imperceptible succession of events; and thus He keeps us always in the darkness of faith. He not only accomplishes His designs gradually, but by means that seem the most simple and the most competent to the end, in order that human wisdom may attribute the success to the means, and thus his own working be less manifest; otherwise, every act of God would seem to be a miracle, and the state of faith, wherein it is the will of God that we should live, would come to an end.

This state of faith is necessary, not only to stimulate the good, causing us to sacrifice our reason in a life so full of darkness, but also to blind us who, by our presumption, deserve such a sentence. We behold the works of God but do not understand them; we can see nothing in them but the effects of material laws. We are destitute of true knowledge, for that is only open to those of us who distrust our own abilities; proud human wisdom is unworthy to be taken into the counsels of God.

God renders the working of grace slow and obscure, that He may keep us in the darkness of faith. He makes use of the inconstancy and ingratitude of the creature, and of the disappointments and surfeits that accompany prosperity, in order to detach us from them both. He frees us from self by revealing to us our weaknesses and our corruptions in a multitude of backslidings. All this dealing appears perfectly natural; and it is by this succession of natural means that we are burned as by a slow fire. We should like to be consumed at once by the flames of pure love; but such an end would scarce cost us anything; it is only an excessive self-love that desires thus to become perfect in a moment and at so cheap a rate.

Why do we rebel against the length of the way? Because we are wrapped up in self, and God must destroy an infatuation that is a constant hindrance to His work. Of what, then, can we complain?

Our trouble is that we are attached to creatures and still more to self. God prepares a series of events that gradually detach us from creatures and separate us from self. The operation is painful but is rendered necessary by our corruption, and the same cause makes it distressing. If our flesh was sound, the surgeon would use no knife; he only cuts in proportion to the depth of the wound and the diseased condition of the parts. Is the surgeon cruel because he cuts to the quick? Nay, on the contrary, he works with both love and skill; he would treat in the same way his only and well-beloved son.

So it is with God. He never afflicts us, if we may so say, except against His own inclination. His paternal heart is not gratified by the sight of our misery, but He cuts to the quick so that He may heal the disease in our souls. He must snatch away from us whatever we cling to too fondly, and all that we love irregularly and to the prejudice of His rights. He acts with us as we do with children; they cry because we take away the knife, which was their amusement, but might have been their death. We weep, we become discouraged, and we cry aloud. We are ready to murmur against God, as children get angry with their mothers. But God lets us weep and secures our salvation; He afflicts only to amend. Even when He seems to overwhelm, He means nothing but good; it is only to spare us the evils we were preparing for ourselves. The things we now lament for a little space would have caused us to mourn forever; what we think lost was indeed lost when we seemed to have it, but now God has laid it aside for us so that we may inherit it in the eternity so near at hand. He deprives us of what we cherish only to teach us how to love it purely, solidly, and moderately, and to secure to us its eternal enjoyment in His own bosom—to do us a thousand times more good than we could ask or think of ourselves.

With the exception of sin, nothing happens in this world out of the will of God. He is the Author, Ruler, and Bestower of all; He has numbered the hairs of our heads, the leaves of every tree, the sand upon the seashore, and the drops of the ocean. When He made the universe, His wisdom weighed and measured every atom. It is He who breathes into us the breath of life and renews it every moment. He knows the number of our days and holds in His all-powerful hand the keys of the tomb to open or to shut.

What we admire is as nothing in the eyes of God; a little more or less of life is a difference that disappears in the light of eternity. What does it matter whether this fragile vessel, this clay tabernacle, is broken and reduced to ashes a little sooner or later?

Ah, what shortsighted and deceitful views are ours! We are thrown into consternation at the death of a man in the prime of life. "What a dreadful loss!" exclaims the world. Who has lost anything? The dead? He has lost some years of vanity, illusion, and danger to his immortal soul; God has snatched him from the midst of his iniquities and separated him from a corrupt world and his own weakness. The friends whom he has left? They are deprived of the poison of worldly felicity; they lose a perpetual intoxication. They get rid of the forgetfulness of God and themselves, in which they lay sunk. Rather, they gain the bliss of detachment from the world through the virtue of the cross. The same blow that saves the dying prepares the survivors by their suffering to labor courageously for their own salvation. O is it not true that God is good, tender, and compassionate toward our misery, even when He seems to launch His thunders at us and we are open-mouthed in our complaints of His severity!

What difference can we discover between two persons who lived a century ago? The one died twenty years before the other, but now they are both gone; the separation that then seemed so abrupt and so long appears as nothing to us, and was, in fact, short. Those things that are severed will soon be reunited, and no trace of the separation will be visible. We look upon ourselves as immortal, or at least as having a duration of ages. O folly and madness! Those who die from day to day tread upon the heels of those who are already dead. Life flows like a torrent, and that which is gone is but a dream. Even while we contemplate that which now is, it vanishes and is lost in the abyss of the past. So will it be with the future. Days, months, and years glide by like the billows of a torrent, each hurrying along after the other. A few moments more and all is over! Alas, how short will that existence then appear which now wearies us with its sad and tedious length!

The disgust of life is the result of the weakness of our self-love. The sick man thinks the night will never end because he sleeps not; but it is no longer than others. We exaggerate all our sufferings by our cowardice. They are great, it is true, but they are magnified by timidity. The way to lessen them is to abandon ourselves courageously into the hands of God. We must suffer, but the end of our pain is to purify our souls and make us worthy of Him.

22

On the Operations of God to Bring Man to the End of His Creation

In the beginning, God attacked us in externals; little by little, He withdrew distractions from His creatures, as we loved them too much, and contrary to His law. But this outward work, though essential in laying the foundation of the building, goes but a little way toward the completion of the whole edifice. The interior operation, although invisible, is beyond comparison—greater, more difficult, and more wonderful!

There comes a time when God, having completely stripped us, having mortified the flesh as to the creatures to which it clung, commences an interior work for the purpose of forcing from us our hold upon self. External objects are now no longer the subjects of His spoliations. He would tear from us the *I* that is the center of our self-love. It was only for the sake of this *I* that we loved all the rest, and He now pursues it relentlessly and without cessation. To deprive a man of his clothing would be harsh treatment enough, but that is nothing in comparison with the discipline that should strip off his skin and muscles and reduce him to a skeleton of bones. Trim up the branches of a tree and, far from killing it, you even add to its vigor, and it shoots out again on every side. But attack the trunk and wither the root, and it fades, languishes, and dies. It is the good will of God toward us, thus, to make us die to self.

As to the external mortification of the senses, He causes us to accomplish it by certain courageous efforts against ourselves. The more the senses are destroyed by the courage of the soul, the more highly does the soul estimate its own virtue and live by its own labor. But in process of time, God reserves for His own hand the work of attacking the soul in its depths and depriving it finally of the last vestige of the life of self. It is no longer the strength of the soul that is then employed against the things without, but its weakness is turned against itself. It looks at self; it is shocked at what it sees. It remains faithful, but it no longer beholds its own fidelity. Every defect in its previous history rises up to view, often including new faults, of which it had never before even suspected the existence. It no longer finds those supports of fervor and courage that formerly nourished it. It faints; like Jesus, it is heavy even unto death. All is taken away but the will to retain nothing, and to let God work without reservation.

It has not even the consolation of perceiving that it has such a will. It is no longer a perceptible, designed will, but is simple, without reflex acts, and so much the more hidden as it is deeper and more intimate in the soul. In such a state, God sees to everything that is necessary to detach the soul from self. He strips it little by little, removing one after another all the investments in which it was wrapped.

The last operations, though not always the greatest, are nevertheless the most severe. Though the outside garments may be more costly than those within, yet the removal of the latter is more painful than that of the former. During the first, we are consoled by reflecting the grosser passions. He attacks all the subtle resources of self-love within, especially in those souls who have generously and without reserve delivered themselves up to the operations of

His grace. The more He would purify them, the more He exercises them interiorly. The world has neither eyes to see nor ears to hear these trials, but the world is blind. Its wisdom is dead; it cannot coexist with the Spirit of truth. Apostle Paul says, *"The things of God knoweth no man, but the Spirit of God"* (1 Corinthians 2:11), and *"the Spirit searcheth...the deep things of God"* (1 Corinthians 2:10).

We are not, at first, accustomed to this interior supervision, which thus tends to raze us to the foundation. We are willing to be silent and recollected, to suffer all things, to be at the disposal of Providence, as a man who passively trusts himself to the current of a river; but we dare not yet risk listening to the interior voice that is calling us to the sacrifices God is preparing. We are like the child Samuel, who did not yet know the Lord; when the Lord called him, he thought it was Eli, but he was told that he had been dreaming and that no one had spoken to him. (See 1 Samuel 3:1–14.) Just so, we are uncertain whether it may not be some imagination that would carry us too far. Often, the high priest Eli, that is, our spiritual advisers, tells us that we have been dreaming and bids us lie down again. But God does not leave us, and continues to wake us until we lend an ear to what He has to say.

If it were a matter of visions, apparitions, revelations, extraordinary illuminations, miracles, or things contrary to true teaching, we should be right in not being detained by them. But when God has led us to a certain point of abandonment, and we subsequently have an interior conviction that He still desires us to give up certain innocent things, the tendency of which is only to make us more simple and more profoundly dead to self, can it be an illusion to yield to such drawings? Probably no one follows them without good counsel. The repugnance that our wisdom and self-love manifest to them is sufficient evidence that they are of grace, for we see that we are only hindered from following them by selfish considerations. The more we fear to do these things, the more we have need to do them, for it is a fear that arises only from delicacy, want of pliability, and attachment either to our pleasures or our views. We must die to all the sentiments of the natural life. Thus, every pretext for retreat is cut off by the conviction in the depths of the soul that the sacrifices required will assist in causing us to die.

Ease and promptness in yielding to these movements are the means by which souls make the greatest advances. Those who are ingenuous enough never to hesitate soon make incredible progress. Others argue and never fail to find a sufficient reason for not following the interior monitor. They are willing and not willing; they want to wait for certainties. They search about for advisers who will bid them not do what they are afraid of doing; they stop at every step and look back, then languish in irresolution and insensibly estrange the Spirit of God. At first they grieve Him by their hesitation; then they irritate Him by formal resistance; and finally they quench His operations by repeated opposition.

While they thus resist, they find pretexts both to conceal and justify the resistance, but they insensibly grow dry. They lose their simplicity and, using what effort they may to deceive themselves, they are not at peace; there is always at the bottom of their conscience a feeling of reproach that they have been wanting toward God. But as God becomes more distant, because they are departing from Him, the soul becomes hardened by degrees. It is no longer peaceful, but it no longer seeks true peace. On the contrary, it wanders farther and farther from it by seeking it where it is not. Like a dislocated bone, a continual source of pain, it is out of its natural position and manifests no tendency to resume its place; on the contrary, it binds itself fast in its false relations.

Ah, how much to be pitied is that soul that is just beginning to reject the secret invitations of God when He demands that it must die to all! At first, it is but an atom, but the atom becomes a mountain and soon forms a sort of chaos between itself and God. We play deaf when God demands a lowly simplicity; we are afraid to listen. We should be glad enough to be able to convince ourselves that we have not heard; we say so, but we are not persuaded. We get into a tumult, we doubt all our past experiences, and the graces that had served the most effectually to make us humble and simple before God begin to look like illusions. We seek without for spiritual advisers who may calm the trouble within; we readily find them, for there are so many, gifted even with much knowledge and piety, who have yet but little experience.

In this condition, the more we strive to recover, the sicker we get. We are as the wounded deer bearing in his side the fatal arrow; the more he struggles through the woods to be delivered of his enemy, the more deeply he buries it in his body. Alas, *"who hath hardened himself against him, and hath prospered?"* (Job 9:4). Can God, who is Himself the true peace, leave that heart peaceful that opposes itself to His designs? Such a person is like one with an unknown disorder. Physicians employ their art in vain to give him any solace. You behold him sad, depressed, languishing. No food and no remedy can avail to do him good; he dies day by day. Can we wonder that, drifting from the true way, we should ceaselessly continue to stray farther and farther from the right course?

But as you will say, the commencement of these things is a small matter. That is true, but the end is deplorable. In the sacrifice that we made when we devoted ourselves wholly to God, we reserved nothing, and felt happy in so doing, while we were looking at things with a general view and at a distance. But when God takes us at our word and accepts our offer in detail, we are made aware of a thousand repugnances, the existence of which we had not so much as suspected before. Our courage fails; frivolous excuses are suggested to flatter our feeble and tempted souls. Then we hesitate and doubt whether it is our duty to obey; we do only half of what God requires of us, and we mix with the divine influence something of self, trying still to secure some nutriment for that corrupt interior that wills not to die. A jealous God retires. The soul begins to shut its eyes, so that it may not see that it no longer has the courage to act; and God leaves it to its weakness and corruption, because it will be so left. But think of the magnitude of its error!

The more we have received of God, the more we ought to render. We have received prevenient love and singular grace; we have received the gift of pure and unselfish love that so many pious souls have never tasted. God has spared nothing to possess us wholly; He has become the interior Bridegroom; He has taken pains to do everything for His bride—but He is infinitely jealous. Do not wonder at the exacting nature of His jealousy! What is its object? Is it talents, illuminations, the regular practice of external virtues? Not at all; He is easy and condescending in such matters. Love is only jealous about love; the whole of His scrutiny falls upon the state of the will. He cannot share the heart of the spouse with any other; still less can He tolerate the excuses by which she would convince herself that her heart is justly divided. This it is that lights the devouring fires of His jealousy. As long, O spouse, as pure and disinterested love will guide you, so long the Bridegroom will bear with inexhaustible patience all your wrongdoing through weakness or inadvertence, without prejudice to the purity of your love. But from the moment that you refuse anything that God asks, and begin to deceive yourself in the refusal, He will regard you as a faithless spouse and one seeking to conceal her infidelity!

How many souls, after having made great sacrifices, fall into these ways! False wisdom is the source of the whole difficulty; it is not so much through defect of courage as through excess of reason that we are arrested at this point. It is true that when God has called souls to this state of absolute sacrifice, He treats them in accordance with the gifts He has lavished upon them. He is insatiable for deaths, losses, and renunciation; He is even jealous of His own gifts, because the excellence of the blessings secretly breeds within us a sort of self-confidence. All must be destroyed; every vestige must perish! We have abandoned everything, and He comes now to take everything, leaving us absolutely nothing. If there be the smallest thing to which we cling, however good it may appear, there He comes, sword in hand, cutting into the remotest corner of the soul. If we are still fearful in any recess, to that spot He comes, for He always attacks us in our weakest points. He pushes hard, without giving us time to breathe. Do you wonder? Can we be dead while we yet breathe? We desire that God would give us the death stroke, but we long to die without pain. We would die to our own will by the power of the will itself; we want to lose all and still hold all. Ah, what agony, what distress, when God has brought us to the end of our strength! We faint like a patient under a painful surgical operation. But the comparison is nothing, for the object of the surgeon is to give us life, that of God is to make us die.

Poor souls, weak in spirit! How these last blows overwhelm you! The very apprehension of them makes you tremble and fall back! How few are there who make out to cross the frightful desert! Scarcely will two or three behold the Promised Land! Woe to those from whom God had reason to expect everything and who do not accept the grace! Woe to him who resists the interior guidance! It is a strange sin, that against the Holy Spirit! Unpardonable in this world and in the next, what is it but resistance to the divine monitor within? He who resists the Spirit, striving for his conversion, will be punished in this world by affliction and in the next by the pains of hell. Happy is he who never hesitates, who fears only that he follows with too little readiness, who would rather do too much against self than too little! Blessed is he who, when asked for a sample, boldly presents his entire stock and suffers God to cut from the whole cloth! Happy is he who, esteeming himself as nothing, puts God to no necessity of sparing him! Thrice happy is he who does this without fear!

It is thought that this state is a painful one; it is a mistake. Here is peace and liberty; here the heart, detached from everything, is immeasurably enlarged so as to become illimitable. Nothing cramps it, and in accordance with the promise, it becomes, in a certain sense, one with God Himself.

You only, O my God, can give the peace that is then enjoyed! The less timid the soul is in the sacrifice of itself, the greater the liberty it does acquire! At length, when it no longer hesitates to lose all and forget self, it possesses all. It is true that it is not a conscious possession, so that the soul addressed itself as happy, for that would be to return to self after having quitted it forever. But it is an image of the condition of the blessed, who will be always ravished by the contemplation of God without having a moment, during the whole of eternity, to think of themselves and their felicity. They are so satisfied in these transports that they will be eternally rejoicing without once saying to themselves that they are happy.

You grant to those souls who never resist You, O Bridegroom of souls, a foretaste of this felicity even in this life. They will all things and nothing. As it is created things that hem up the heart, these souls, being restrained by no attachment to the creature and no reflections of self, enter as it were into Your immensity! Nothing stops them; they become continually more and more lost, but though their capacity should increase to an infinite extent, You would fill it. They are always satisfied. They do not say that they are happy but feel that they are so; they do not possess happiness, but their happiness possesses them. Let anyone ask them at any moment, "Do you will to suffer what you suffer? Would you have what you have not?" They will answer without hesitation and without reflection, "I will to suffer what I suffer and to want that which I have not. I will everything that God wills; I will nothing else."

Such, my God, is true and pure worship in spirit and in truth. You seek such to worship You but scarce find them! There are few who do not seek self in Your gifts, but instead seek You alone in the cross and in spoliation. Most seek to guide You instead of being guided by You. They give themselves up to You so that they may become great, but withdraw when they are required to become little. They say they are attached to nothing and are overwhelmed by the smallest losses. They desire to possess You but are not willing to lose self so that they may be possessed by You. This is not loving You; it is desiring to be loved by You. O God, the creature knows not to what end You have made him. Teach him and write in the depths of his soul, so that the clay must suffer itself to be shaped at the will of the Potter!

23

On Christian Perfection

Christian perfection is not that rigorous, tedious, cramping thing that many imagine. It demands only an entire surrender of everything to God from the depths of the soul; and the moment this takes place, whatever is done for Him becomes easy. Those who are God's without reserve are in every state content, for they will only what He wills and desire to do for Him whatever He desires them to do. They strip themselves of everything, and in this nakedness, they find all things restored a hundredfold. Peace of conscience, liberty of spirit, the sweet abandonment of themselves and theirs into the hand of God, the joy of perceiving the light always increasing in their hearts, and finally the freedom of their souls from the bondage of the fears and desires of this world—these things constitute that return of happiness that the true children of God receive a hundredfold in the midst of their crosses while they remain faithful.

They are sacrificed, it is true, but it is to Him whom they love best; they suffer, but they will to endure all that they do receive, and they prefer that anguish to all the false joys of the world. Their bodies are subject to excruciating pain, their imaginations are troubled, and their minds become languid and weak, but the will is firm and peacefully quiet in the interior of the soul, and it responds with a joyful *amen* to every stroke from the hand that would perfect the sacrifice.

What God requires of us is a will that is no longer divided between He and any creature—a simple, pliable state of will that desires what He desires, rejects nothing but what He rejects, wills without reserve what He wills, and under no pretext wills what He does not. In this state of mind, all things are proper for us; our amusements, even, are acceptable in His sight.

Blessed is he who thus gives himself to God! He is delivered from his passions, from the opinions of men, from their malice, from the tyranny of their maxims, from their cold and miserable raillery, from the misfortunes that the world attributes to chance, from the infidelity and fickleness of friends, from the artifices and snares of enemies, from the wretchedness and shortness of life, from the horrors of an ungodly death, from the cruel remorse that follows sinful pleasures, and finally from the everlasting condemnation of God!

The true Christian is delivered from this innumerable multitude of evils because, putting his will into the hands of God, he wills only what He wills, and thus he finds comfort in the midst of all his suffering in the way of faith and its attendant hope.

What weakness it is, then, to be fearful of consecrating ourselves to God and of getting too far into so desirable a state! Happy are those who throw themselves, as it were, headlong, and, with their eyes shut, into the arms of "*the Father of mercies, and the God of all comfort*" (2 Corinthians 1:3). Their whole desire, then, is to know what the will of God is for them, and they fear nothing so much as not perceiving the whole of His requirements. As soon as they behold a new light in His law, they are transported with joy, like a miser at the finding of a treasure.

No matter what cross may overwhelm the true child of God, he wills everything that happens and would not have anything removed that his Father appoints; the more he loves God, the more he is filled with content. And the most stringent perfection, far from being a burden, only renders his yoke the lighter.

What folly it is to fear being too devoted to God! To fear being happy! To fear loving the will of God in all things! To fear having too much courage under inevitable crosses, too much consolation in the love of God, and too great a detachment from the passions that make us miserable!

Let us refuse, then, to set our affections upon things of the earth, so that we may set them exclusively upon God. I do not say that we must abandon them entirely, for if our lives are already moral and well ordered, we have only to change the secret motive of our actions into love, and we may continue almost the same course of life. God does not overturn our conditions or the duties attached to them, but we may go on doing now for the service of God that which we did formerly to satisfy the world and to please ourselves. There will be this difference only: Instead of being harassed by pride, by overbearing passion, and by the malicious censures of the world, we will act with liberty, with courage, and with hope in God. We will be animated with confidence; the expectation of things eternal, which advance as things temporal recede from us, will support us in the midst of suffering. The love of God, who will cause us to perceive how great His love is toward us, will lend us wings to fly in His ways and to raise us above all our miseries. Is this hard to believe? Experience will convince us. *"O taste and see that the Lord is good"* (Psalm 34:8), says the psalmist.

The Son of God says to every Christian without exception, *"If any man will come after me, let him deny himself, and take up his cross, and follow me"* (Matthew 16:24). The broad way leads to destruction; we must walk in the straight way, though there are few who travel there. It is only the violent who take the kingdom by force. (See Matthew 11:12.) We must be born again, renounce and hate ourselves, become children, be poor in spirit, mourn that we may be comforted, and not be of this world, which is cursed because of offenses.

Many are afraid of these truths, and their fear arises from this—that while they know the exacting nature of religion, they are ignorant of its gifts and of the Spirit of love that renders everything easy. They are not aware that religion leads to the highest perfection, while bestowing peace through a principle of love that smooths every rough place.

Those who are in truth and indeed wholly consecrated to God are ever happy. They prove that the yoke of our Redeemer is easy and His burden light, that in Him is the peace of the soul, and that He gives rest to those who are weary and heavy laden, according to His own blessed promise. But how unhappy are those poor, weak souls who are divided between God and the world! They will and they do not will; they are lacerated at once by their passions and their remorse; they are afraid of the judgments of God and of the opinions of men; they dislike the evil but are ashamed of the good; they suffer the pains of virtue without enjoying its consolations. Ah, could they but have a little courage, just enough to despise the vain conversation, the cold sneers, and the rash judgments of men, what peace would they not enjoy in the bosom of God!

It is dangerous to our salvation, unworthy of God and of us, and destructive even to our peace of mind to desire to remain always in our present position. Our whole lives are only given to us that we may advance with rapid strides toward our heavenly country. The world recedes like a deceptive shadow, and eternity already approaches to receive us. Why do we linger and look behind while the light of the Father of mercies is shining upon us from before? Let us make haste to reach the kingdom of God.

All the vain pretexts that are used to cover our reservations toward God are instantly dissipated by the first commandment of the law: "*Thou shalt love the Lord thy God with all thy heart, and with all thy soul, and with all thy strength, and with all thy mind"* (Luke 10:27). Notice how many expressions are here brought together by the Holy Spirit to forestall all the reservations the soul might make to the prejudice of this jealous love—not only with the whole extent and strength of the soul but with all the intensity of the intellect. How, then, can we conclude that we love Him if we cannot make up our minds to receive His law and to apply ourselves at once to fulfill all His blessed will?

Those who fear that they will discover too clearly what this love demands are very far indeed from possessing the active and incessant affection required by this commandment. There is only one way in which God should be loved, and that is to take no step except with Him and for Him, and to follow, with a generous self-abandonment, everything that He requires.

Those who live in some self-denial but still have a wish to enjoy a little of the world think that this is a small matter, but they run the risk of being included in the number of those lukewarm ones whom God will spew out of His mouth. (See Revelation 3:16.)

God is not pleased with the souls who say, "Thus far will I go and no farther." Should the creature prescribe laws to the Creator? What would a master say of his servants, or a king of his subjects, if they were willing to serve him, but only after their own fashion; if they were afraid of becoming too much interested in his service and his interests; if they were ashamed to publicly acknowledge themselves as being attached to him? Or rather, what will the King of Kings say to us if we serve Him in this wicked manner?

The time is not far-off. It is near; it is even at hand. Let us hasten to anticipate it, and let us love that eternal beauty that never grows old, and that preserves in endless youth those who love nothing but it. Let us despise this miserable world that is already falling to pieces on every side! Have we not seen for years that those who are high in honor and in the esteem of men today are surprised by death and laid side by side in the tomb tomorrow?

This poor world, the object of so much insane attachment, we are daily about to leave; it is but misery, vanity, and folly; a phantom, the very fashion of which passes away. (See 1 Corinthians 7:31.)

24

On Naked Faith and Pure Love

Those who are attached to God only insofar as they enjoy pleasure and consolation resemble those who followed the Lord not to hear His teaching but because they ate of the loaves and were filled. (See John 6:26.) They are ready to say with Peter, "*Master, it is good for us to be here: and let us make three tabernacles*" (Mark 9:5), but they know not what they say. After being intoxicated with the joys of the mountain, they deny the Son of God and refuse to follow Him to Calvary. Not only do they desire delights, but they seek illuminations also. The mind is curious to behold, while the heart requires to be filled with soft and flattering emotions. Is this dying to self? Is this the way in which the just live by faith? (See Hebrews 10:38.)

They desire to have extraordinary revelations that may be regarded as supernatural gifts and a mark of the special favor of God. Nothing is as flattering to self-love. All the greatness of the world at once could not so inflate the heart. These supernatural gifts nourish in secret the life of nature. It is an ambition of the most refined character, as it is wholly spiritual, but it is merely ambition—a desire to feel, to enjoy, to possess God and His gifts, to behold His light, to discern spirits, and to prophesy—in short, to be an extraordinarily gifted person. For the enjoyment of illuminations and delights leads the soul little by little toward a secret coveting of all these things.

Yet the apostle shows us a more excellent way (see 1 Corinthians 12:31), for which he inspires us with a holy emulation; it is the way of love that seeks not her own (see 1 Corinthians 13:5) and desires not to be adorned (if we may adopt the apostle's language), but allows herself to be unclothed. She is less in search of pleasure than of God, whose will she longs to fulfill. If she finds pleasure in devotion, she does not rest in it, but makes it serve to strengthen her weakness, as a convalescent uses a staff to aid in walking, but throws it aside on his restoration. In the same way, the tender and childlike soul that God fed with milk in the beginning suffers itself to be weaned when He sees it is time that it should be nourished upon strong meat.

We must not be ever children, always hanging upon the breast of heavenly consolations; we must put away childish things, along with Saint Paul. (See 1 Corinthians 13:11.) Our early joys were excellent to attract us, to detach us from gross and worldly pleasures by others of a purer kind, and to lead us into a life of prayer and recollection. But to be constantly in a state of enjoyment that takes away the feeling of the cross, and to live in a passionate devotion that continually keeps paradise open—this is not dying upon the cross and becoming nothing.

This life of illumination and sensible delights is a very dangerous snare if we become so attached to it as to desire nothing further; for he who has no other attraction to prayer will quit both it and God whenever this source of his gratification is dried up. Saint Teresa says, you know, that a vast number of souls leave off praying at the very moment when their devotion is beginning to be real. How many are there who, in consequence of too tender rearing in Jesus Christ and too great fondness for the milk of His Word, go back and abandon the interior life as soon as God undertakes to wean them! We need not be astonished at this, for they mistake the portico of the temple for the very sanctuary itself; they desire the death of their gross external passions so that they may lead a delicious life of self-satisfaction within. Hence so much infidelity and disappointment, even among those who appeared to be the most fervent and the most devoted. Those who have talked the loudest of abandonment, of death to self, of the darkness of faith, and of desolation are often the most surprised and discouraged when they really experience these things, and their consolation is taken away. O how excellent is the way pointed out by John of the cross; Jesus would have us believe without seeing and love without desiring to feel! (See John 20:29.)

This attachment to sensible delights is the fruitful source of all our illusions; souls are earthly in desiring something tangible, as it were, before they can feel firm. But this is all wrong; it is these very things of sense that produce vacillation. We think that while the pleasure lasts, we will never desert God; we say in our prosperity that we will never be moved. (See Psalm 30:6.) But the moment our intoxication is over, we give up all for lost, thus substituting our own pleasure and imagination in place of God. Naked faith, alone, is a sure guard against illusion. When our foundation is not upon any imagination, feeling, pleasure, or extraordinary illumination—when we rest upon God only in pure and naked faith, in the simplicity of the gospel; receive the consolations that He sends but dwell in none; abstain from judging and be ever obedient; believe that it is easy to be deceived and that others may be able to set us right; in short, acting every moment with simplicity and an upright intention, and following the light of the faith of the present moment—then we are indeed in a way that is but little subject to illusion.

Experience will demonstrate, better than anything else, how much more certain this path is than that of illuminations and sensible delights. Whoever will try it will soon find that this way of naked faith, rigidly followed, is the profoundest and most complete death of self. Interior delights and revelations indemnify our self-love for all its external sacrifices, and cherish a secret and refined life of nature; but to suffer ourselves to be stripped within and without at once (without by Providence and within by the night of pure faith), this is a total sacrifice and a state that is furthest from self-deception.

Those, then, who seek to guard against being deceived by a constant succession of emotions and certainties are by that very course exposing themselves most surely to such a result. On the other hand, those who follow the leadings of the love that strips them and the faith that walks in darkness, without seeking any other support, avoid all the sources of error and illusion. The author of the *Imitation of Christ* (book 3) tells you that if God takes away your inward delights, it should be your pleasure to remain pleasureless. O how beloved of God is a soul thus crucified, who rests calmly upon the cross and desires only to expire with Jesus! It is not true to say that we are afraid of having lost God when being deprived of feeling; it is impatience under the trial, the restlessness of a pampered and dainty nature, a search for some support for self-love, a weariness of abandonment, and a secret return to self after our consecration to God. O God, where are those who stop not in the road to death? If they persevere to the end, they will receive a crown of life.

25

On the Presence of God

The true source of all our perfection is contained in the command of God to Abraham: *"Walk before me, and be thou perfect"* (Genesis 17:1).

The presence of God calms the soul and gives it quiet and repose even during the day and in the midst of occupation—but we must be given up to God without reserve.

When we have once found God, we have nothing to seek among men; we must make the sacrifice of our dearest friendships; the best of friends has entered into our hearts, that jealous Bridegroom who requires the whole of it for Himself.

It takes no great time to love God, to be refreshed by His presence, to elevate our hearts to Him, to worship Him in the depths of our souls, or to offer to Him all we do and all we suffer; this is the true kingdom of God within us, which cannot be disturbed.

When the distraction of the senses and the vivacity of the imagination hinder the soul from a sweet and peaceful state of recollection, we should at least be calm as to the state of the will. In that case, the will to be recollected is a sufficient state of recollection for the time being. We must return to God and do everything He would have us do with a right intention. We must endeavor to awake within ourselves, from time to time, the desire of being devoted to God in all the extent of our powers—in our intellect, to know Him and think on Him, and in our will, to love Him. We must desire, too, that our outward senses may be consecrated to Him in all their operations.

Let us be careful how we voluntarily engage, either externally or internally, in matters that cause such distraction of the will and intellect and so draw them out of themselves so that they find difficulty in re-entering and finding God. The moment we discover that anything causes excessive pleasure or joy within us, let us separate our hearts from it, and, to prevent it from seeking its repose in the creature, let us present it to God, the true object of love, the sovereign good. If we are faithful in breaking up all attachment to the creature, that is, if we prevent its entering into those depths of the soul that our Lord reserves for Himself, to dwell there and to be there respected, adored, and loved, we will soon experience that pure joy that He never fails to give to a soul freed and detached from all human affections.[3]

Whenever we perceive within us anxious desires for anything, whatever it may be, and find that nature is hurrying us with too much haste to do what is to be done, whether it be to say something, see something, or to do something, let us stop short and repress the precipitancy of our thoughts and the agitation of our actions—for God has said that His Spirit does not dwell in disquiet.

Be careful not to take too much interest in what is going on around you or to be much engaged in it; it is a fruitful source of distraction. As soon as we have found what it is that God requires of us in anything that comes up, let us stop there and separate ourselves from all the rest. By that means, we will always preserve

3. Note from the editor: The reader will not understand by this, that the soul, in a state of true abandonment, does not exhibit affection for those about it. As, by that process, it commences to see God as He is, and it also begins to be like Him, and is all love. Its whole existence, like that of God, may be summed up in the single word *love*. But its love is divine, not human; its affection for all creatures of God, in their respective relations, is higher and deeper and holier than it ever was before.

the depths of the free and equable soul and rid ourselves of many things that embarrass our hearts and prevent them from turning easily toward God.

An excellent means of preserving our interior solitude and liberty of soul is to make it a rule to put an end to, at the close of every action, all reflections upon it and all reflex acts of self-love, whether of a vain joy or sorrow. Happy is he whose mind contains only what is necessary, and who thinks of nothing except when it is time to think of it! So it is God who excites the impression, by calling us to perform His will as soon as it is exhibited, rather than the mind laboriously foreseeing and seeking it. In short, let us be accustomed to recollect ourselves during the day, and in the midst of our occupations, by a simple view of God. Let us silence by that means all the movements of our hearts when they appear in the least agitated. Let us separate ourselves from all that does not come from God. Let us suppress our superfluous thoughts and reveries. Let us utter no useless word. Let us seek God within us, and we will find Him without fail, and with Him, joy and peace.

While outwardly busy, let us be more occupied with God than with everything and everyone else. To be rightly engaged, we must be in His presence and employed for Him. At the sight of the majesty of God, our interior ought to become calm and remain tranquil. Once a single word of the Savior suddenly calmed a furiously agitated sea. (See Matthew 8:26; Mark 4:39.) One look of His at us, and of ours toward Him, ought always to perform the same miracle within us.

We must often raise our hearts to God. He will purify, enlighten, and direct them. Such was the daily practice of the sacred psalmist: "*I have set the* Lord *always before me*" (Psalm 16:8). Let us often employ the beautiful words of the same holy prophet: "*Whom have I in heaven but thee? And there is none upon earth that I desire beside thee!…God is the strength of my heart, and my portion for ever!"* (Psalm 73:25–26).

We must not wait for a leisure hour when we can bar our doors; the moment that is employed in regretting that we have no opportunity to be recollected might be profitably spent in recollection. Let us turn our hearts toward God in a simple, familiar spirit, full of confidence in Him. The most interrupted moments, even while eating or listening to others, are valuable. Tiresome and idle talk in our presence, instead of annoying talk, will afford us the delight of employing the interval in seeking God. Thus all things work together for good to those who love God. (See Romans 8:28.)

We must read according to our necessity, and desire, but with frequent interruptions, for the purpose of recollection. A word or two, simple and full of the Spirit of God, will be to us as hidden manna. We forget the words, but the effect remains; they operate in secret, and the soul is fed and enriched.

26

On Conformity to the Will of God

The essence of virtue consists in the attitude of the will. This is what the Lord would teach us when He said, *"The kingdom of God is within you"* (Luke 17:21). It is not a question of extensive knowledge, of splendid talents, or even of great deeds; it is a simple matter of having a heart and loving. Outward works are the fruits and consequences of loving, and the spring of all good things is at the bottom of the soul.

There are some virtues that are appropriate to certain conditions and not to others; some are good at one time and some at another, but an upright will is profitable for all times and all places. That kingdom of God that is within us consists in our willing whatever God wills, always, in everything, and without reservation. And thus His kingdom comes, for His will is then done as it is in heaven, since we will nothing but what is dictated by His sovereign pleasure.

Blessed are the poor in spirit! Blessed are those who are stripped of everything, even of their own wills, so that they may no longer belong to themselves! How poor in spirit does a person become who has given up all things to God! But how is it that our will becomes right when it unreservedly conforms to that of God? We will whatever He wills; what He does not will, we do not. We attach our feeble wills to that all-powerful One, who regulates everything. Thus, nothing can ever come to pass against our wishes, for nothing can happen contrary to the will of God; and we find in His good pleasure an inexhaustible source of peace and consolation.

The interior life is the beginning of the blessed peace of the saints, who eternally cry, "Amen, Amen! We adore, we praise, we bless God in everything; we see Him incessantly, and in all things, His paternal hand is the sole object of our contemplation. There are no longer any evils, for even the most terrible things that come upon us work together for good, as Saint Paul says, for those who love God. (See Romans 8:28.) Can the suffering that God destines to purify us and make us worthy of Himself be called an evil?

Let us cast all our cares, then, into the bosom of so good a Father and suffer Him to do as He pleases. Let us be content to adopt His will in all points and to abandon our own, absolutely and forever. How can we retain anything of our own when we do not even belong to ourselves? The slave has nothing; how much less, then, should we own anything, we who in ourselves are but nothingness and sin, and who are indebted for everything to pure grace! God has only bestowed upon us a will, free and capable of self-possession, that we may the more generously recompense the gift by returning it to its rightful owner.

We have nothing but our wills only; all the rest belongs elsewhere. Disease removes life and health; riches make to themselves wings; intellectual talents depend upon the state of the body. The only thing that really belongs to us is our will; and it is of this, therefore, that God is especially jealous, for He gave it to us, not that we should retain it, but that we should return it to Him, whole as we received it, and without the slightest reservation.

If the least desire or the smallest hesitation remains, it is robbing God, contrary to the order of creation, for all things come from Him, and to Him they are all due.

Alas, how many souls are full of self and desirous of doing good and serving God, but in such a way as to suit themselves. They desire to impose rules upon God as to His manner of drawing them to Himself. They want to serve and possess Him, but they are not willing to abandon themselves to Him and be possessed by Him.

What a resistance they offer to Him, even when they appear so full of zeal and fervor! It is certain that, in one sense, their spiritual abundance becomes an obstacle to their progress, for they hold it all, even their virtues, in appropriation and constantly seek self, even in good. O how superior to such fervid and illuminated souls, walking always in virtue, in a road of their own choice, is that humble heart that renounces its own life and every selfish movement, and dismisses all will except such as God gives from moment to moment, in accordance with His gospel and providence!

Herein lies the meaning of those words of the Lord: *"If any man will come after me, let him deny himself, and take up his cross, and follow me"* (Matthew 16:24; see also Luke 14:33). We must follow Jesus Christ step-by-step and not open up a path for ourselves. We can only follow Him by denying ourselves, and what is this but unreservedly abandoning every right over ourselves? And so Saint Paul tells us, *"Ye are not your own"* (1 Corinthians 6:19). No, not a thing remains that belongs to us! Alas for him who resumes possession of anything after once abandoning it!

To desire to serve God in one place rather than in another, in this way rather than in that—is not this desiring to serve Him in our own way rather than in His? But to be equally ready for all things; to will everything and nothing; to leave ourselves in His hands, like a toy in the hands of a child; to set no bounds to our abandonment, inasmuch as the perfect reign of God cannot abide them—this is really denying ourselves. This is treating Him like God, and ourselves like creatures made solely for His use.

27

On General Directions for Attaining Inward Peace

There is no peace for those who resist God; if there is joy in the world, it is reserved for a pure conscience. The whole earth is full of tribulation and anguish for those who do not possess it.

How different is the peace of God from that of the world! It calms the passions, preserves the purity of the conscience, is inseparable from righteousness, unites us to God, and strengthens us against temptations. The peace of the soul consists in an absolute resignation to the will of God.

"Martha, Martha, thou art careful and troubled about many things: But one thing is needful" (Luke 10:41–42). The pain we suffer from so many occurrences arises from the fact that we are not entirely abandoned to God in everything that happens.

Let us put all things, then, into His hands and offer them to Him in our hearts as a sacrifice beforehand. From the moment that you cease to desire anything according to your own judgment, and begin to will everything just as God wills it, you will be free from your former tormenting reflections and anxieties about your own concerns; you will no longer have anything to conceal or take care of.

Until then, you will be troubled, vacillating in your views and enjoyments, easily dissatisfied with others, little satisfied with yourself, and full of reserve and distrust. Your good intentions, until they become truly humble and simple, will only torment you; your piety, however sincere, will be the occasion of more internal reproach then of support or consolation. But if you will abandon your whole heart to God, you will be full of peace and joy in the Holy Ghost.

Alas for you if you will regard man in the work of God! In our choice of a guide, men must be counted as nothing; the slightest respect for their opinion dries up the stream of grace and increases our indecision. We suffer, and we displease God besides.

How can we refuse to bestow all our love upon God, who first loved us with the tender love of a Father, pitying our frailty, and well knowing the mire from which we have been dragged? When a soul is filled with this love, it enjoys peace of conscience; it is content and happy, and it does not require greatness or reputation or pleasure or any of the perishing gifts of time. It desires only the will of God and watches incessantly in the joyful expectation of its Spouse.

28

On Pure Love and Sufferings

We know that we must suffer and that we deserve it; nevertheless, we are always surprised at affliction, as if we thought we neither merited it nor had need of it. It is only true, and pure love that delights to endure for nothing else is perfectly abandoned. Resignation induces us to bear pain, but there is a something in it that is afflicted in suffering and resists. The resignation that measures out its abandonment to God with selfish reflection is willing to suffer, but is constantly examining to ascertain whether it suffers acceptably. In fact, the resigned soul is composed as it were of two persons—one keeping the other in subjection and watching lest it should revolt.

In pure love, unselfish and abandoned, the soul is fed in silence on the cross and on union with the crucified Savior, without any reflections on the severity of its sufferings. There exists but a single, simple will that permits God to see it just as it is, without endeavoring to behold itself. It says nothing, does nothing. What then does it do? It suffers. And is this all? Yes, all; it has nothing else to do but to suffer. Love can be heard easily enough without speech or thought. It does all that it is required to do, which is to have no will when it is stripped of all consolation. The purest of all loves is a will so filled with that of God that there remains nothing else.

What a consolation is it to think that we are then rid of so many anxieties about our exercise of patience and the other virtues in the sight of those about us? It is enough to be humbled and abandoned in the midst of suffering. This is not courage; it is something both less and more—less in the eyes of the ordinary class of Christians and more in the eyes of pure faith. It is a humiliation that raises the soul into all the greatness of God; a weakness that strips it of every resource to bestow upon it His omnipotence. "*When I am weak,*" says Saint Paul, "*then am I strong*" (2 Corinthians 12:10); "*I can do all things through Christ which strengtheneth me*" (Philippians 4:13).

It suffices, then, to feed upon some short sentences suited to our state and our taste, with frequent interruptions to quiet the senses and make room for the inward spirit of recollection. We sometimes suffer, scarcely knowing that we are in distress; at other times, we suffer and know that we bear it ill, but we carry this second and heavier cross without impatience. True love goes ever straightforward, not in its own strength, but esteeming itself as nothing. Then, indeed, we are truly happy. The cross is no longer a cross when there is no self to suffer under it and to appropriate its good and evil.

29

On Interested and Disinterested Love

Why do the gifts of God confer more pleasure when they exist in ourselves than when they are conferred upon our neighbor if we are not attached to self? If we prefer to see them in our possession rather than in that of those about us, we will certainly be afflicted when we see them more perfect in them than they are in ourselves, and this constitutes envy. What is our duty then? We must rejoice that the will of God is done in us and that it reigns there not for our happiness and perfection but for His own good pleasure and glory.

Now, take notice of two matters. The first is that this distinction is not an empty subtlety, for God, in His desire to desolate the soul for its own perfection, causes it really to pass through these trials of self, and He never lets it alone until He has deprived its love of selfish reflection and support. There is nothing as jealous, as exacting, and as searching as this principle of pure love; it cannot abide a thousand things that were imperceptible in our previous state, and what pious persons would call an unprofitable nicety seems an essential point to the soul that is desirous of destroying self. As with gold in the furnace, the fire consumes all that is not gold. So it seems necessary that the heart should be melted with fervent heat so that the love of God may be rendered pure.

The second remark is that God does not pursue every soul in this way in the present life. There is an infinite number of truly pious persons whom He leaves in some degree under the dominion of self-love; these remains of self help to support them in the practice of virtue and serve to purify them to a certain point.

Scarce anything would be more injudicious or more dangerous than to deprive them of the contemplation of the grace of God in them as tending to their own personal perfection. The first class exercise disinterested gratitude; they are thankful to God for whatever He does in them solely because He does it for His own glory; the second are also grateful, but partly because their own perfection is secured at the same time. If the former should endeavor to deprive the latter of this mixed motive and this interior comfort in self, in reference to grace, they would cause them as much injury as they would an infant by weaning it before it was able to eat. To take away the breast would be to destroy it. We must never seek to deprive a soul of the food that still contains nutriment for it, and that God suffers to remain as a stay to its weakness. To obstruct grace is to destroy it.

Neither must the latter condemn the former because they do not see them as much concerned as themselves about their own perfection in the grace ministered unto them. God works in every one as He pleases: *"The wind bloweth where it listeth"* (John 3:8), and *as* it listeth. The forgetfulness of self in the pure contemplation of God is a state in which God can do in our souls whatever most pleases Himself. The important point is that those who are still in a measure supported by self should not be too anxious about the state of such as are in pure love; neither should these latter endeavor to make the former pass through the trials peculiar to a higher state of grace before God calls them to it.

30

On True Liberty

When we are no longer embarrassed by the restless reflections of self, we begin to enjoy true liberty.

False wisdom, on the other hand, is always on the watch, ever occupied with self, constantly jealous of its own perfection, and suffers severely whenever it is permitted to perceive the smallest speck of imperfection.

Not that the man who is simpleminded and detached from self fails to labor toward the attainment of perfection; he is the more successful in proportion as he forgets himself and never dreams of virtue in any other light than as something that accomplishes the will of God.

The source of all our defects is the love of self; we refer everything to that instead of to the love of God. Whoever, then, will labor to get rid of self, to deny him*self*, according to the instructions of Christ, strikes at once at the root of every evil, and finds, in this simple abandonment of self, the germ of every good.

Then the words of Scripture are heard within and understood: "*Where the Spirit of the Lord is, there is liberty*" (2 Corinthians 3:17). We neglect nothing to cause the kingdom of God to come both within and without, but in the midst of our frailties, we are at peace. We would rather die than commit the slightest voluntary sin, but we have no fear for our reputation from the judgment of man. We court the reproach of Christ Jesus and dwell in peace though surrounded by uncertainties. The judgments of God do not frighten us, for we abandon ourselves to them, imploring His mercy according to our attainments in confidence, sacrifice, and absolute surrender. The greater the abandonments, the more flowing the peace; and it sets us in such a large place that we are prepared for everything. We will everything and nothing; we are as guileless as babes.

Our illumination from God discovers the lightest transgressions but never discourages. We walk before Him, but if we stumble, we hasten to resume our way and have no watchword but *onward*!

If we would find God, we must destroy the remains of the old Adam within. The Lord held a little child in His arms when He declared, *"Of such is the kingdom of heaven"* (Matthew 19:14). The sum of the principal directions is this: Do not reason too much, always have an upright purpose in the smallest matters, and pay no attention to the thousand reflections by which we wrap and bury ourselves in self, under pretence of correcting our faults.

31

On the Employment of Time

I understand perfectly well that you do not ask at my hands any proof that it is incumbent upon us to employ all our time to good purpose; grace has long since convinced you of this. It is a pleasant thing to come in contact with those who can meet us halfway. But notwithstanding this, much remains to be done, and there is a wonderful distance between the conviction of the intellect, even combined with the good intention of the heart, and a faithful and exact obedience.

Nothing has been more common in ancient, as well as in modern, times, than to meet souls who were perfect and holy, theoretically. "*Ye shall know them by their fruits*" (Matthew 7:16), says the Savior. And this is the only rule that never deceives when it is properly understood; it is that by which we must judge ourselves.

There is a time for everything in our lives, but the maxim that governs every moment is that there should be none useless, that they should all enter into the order and sequence of our salvation, that they are all accompanied by duties that God has allotted with His own hand, and of which He will demand an account. For from the first instant of our existence to the last, He has never assigned us a barren moment, nor one that we can consider as given up to our own discretion. The great thing is to recognize His will in relation to them. This is to be effected, not by an eager and restless seeking, which is much more likely to spoil everything than to enlighten us as to our duty, but by a true submission to those whom God has set over us, and having a pure and upright heart that seeks God in its simplicity and heartily opposes all the duplicity and false wisdom of self as fast as it is revealed. For we misemploy our time, not only when we do wrong or do nothing, but also when we do something else than what was incumbent on us at the moment, even though it may be the means of good. We are strangely ingenious in perpetually seeking our own interest, and what the world does nakedly and without shame, those who desire to be devoted to God do also, but in a refined manner, under favor of some pretext that serves as a veil to hide from them the deformity of their conduct.

The best general means to ensure the profitable employment of our time is to accustom ourselves to living in continual dependence upon the Spirit of God and His law—receiving every instant whatever He is pleased to bestow, consulting Him in every emergency requiring instant action, having recourse to Him in our weaker moments (when virtue seems to fail), and invoking His aid and rising our hearts to Him whenever we are solicited by sensible objects and find ourselves surprised and estranged from God and far from the true road.

Happy is the soul who commits itself, by a sincere self-abandonment, into the hands of its Creator, ready to do all His will and continually crying, "Lord, what would You have me do?" "*Teach me to do thy will; for thou art my God*" (Psalm 143:10).

During our necessary occupations, we need only pay a simple attention to the leadings of Divine Providence. As they are all prepared for us and presented by Him, our only care should be to receive them with a childlike spirit and submit everything absolutely to Him—our temper, our own will, our scruples, our restlessness, our self-reflections, and our overflowing emotions of hurry, vain joy, or other passions that assault us as we are pleased or displeased with the different events of the day. Let us be careful, however, not to suffer ourselves to be overwhelmed by the multiplicity of our exterior occupations, be they what they may.

Let us endeavor to commence every enterprise with a pure view to the glory of God, continue it without distraction, and finish it without impatience.

The intervals of relaxation and amusement are the most dangerous seasons for us and perhaps the most useful for others; we must, then, be on our guard, that we be as faithful as possible to the presence of God. We must make use of all that Christian vigilance so much recommended by our Lord, raise our hearts to God in the simple view of faith, and dwell in sweet and peaceful dependence upon the Spirit of grace as the only means of our safety and strength. This is especially necessary for those who are looked up to as being in authority and whose words may be the cause of so much good or evil.

Our leisure hours are ordinarily the sweetest and pleasantest for ourselves; we can never employ them better than in refreshing our spiritual strength by a secret and intimate communion with God. Prayer is so necessary and the source of so many blessings that he who has discovered the treasure cannot be prevented from having recourse to it whenever he has an opportunity.

I could add much more concerning these matters, and I may perhaps do so if my present views do not escape me, but if they do, it is of little consequence. God gives others when He pleases; if He does not, it is a proof that they are not necessary, and if that is the case, we should be well satisfied with their loss.

Spiritual Letters

By François Fénelon

"And I have declared unto them thy name, and will declare it: that the love wherewith thou hast loved me may be in them, and I in them."

—John 17:26

Contents

Letter 1: The Advantage of Humiliation

I pray often to God that He would keep you in the hollow of His hand. The most essential point is lowliness. It is profitable for all things, for it produces a teachable spirit, which makes everything easy. You would be more guilty than many others if you made any resistance to God on this point. On the one hand, you have received abundant light and grace on the necessity of becoming like a little child, and on the other, no one has had an experience fitter to humiliate the heart and destroy self-confidence. The great profit to be derived from an experience of our weakness is to render us lowly and obedient. May the Lord keep you!

Letter 2: How to Bear Suffering to Preserve Our Peace

As to our friend, I pray God to bestow upon him a simplicity that will give him peace. When we are faithful in instantly dropping all superfluous and restless reflections, which arise from a self-love as different as possible from charity, we will be set in a large place even in the midst of the straight and narrow path. We will be in the pure liberty and innocent peace of the children of God, without being found wanting either toward God or man.

I apply to myself the same counsel that I give to others, and I am well persuaded that I must seek my own peace in the same direction. My heart is now suffering, but it is the life of self that causes us pain. That which is dead does not suffer. If we were dead and our lives were hidden with Christ in God (see Colossians 3:3), we should no longer perceive those pains in spirit that now afflict us. We should not only bear bodily sufferings with equanimity, but also spiritual affliction—that is to say, trouble sent upon the soul without its own immediate act. But the disturbances of a restless activity, in which the soul adds the burden of an agitated resistance and an unwillingness to suffer to the cross imposed by the hand of God, are only experienced in consequence of the remaining life of self.

A cross that comes purely from God and is cordially welcomed without any self-reflective acts is at once painful and peaceful. But one unwillingly received and repelled by the life of nature is doubly severe; the resistance within is harder to bear than the cross itself. If we recognize the hand of God and make no opposition in the will, we have comfort in our affliction. Happy indeed are those who can bear their sufferings in the enjoyment of this simple peace and perfect acquiescence in the will of God! Nothing shortens and soothes our pains as this spirit of non-resistance.

But we are generally desirous of bargaining with God; we would like at least to impose the limits and see the end of our sufferings. That same obstinate and hidden hold of life, which renders the cross necessary, causes us to reject it in part, and by a secret resistance that impairs its virtue. We have thus to go over the same ground again and again; we suffer greatly but to very little purpose. The Lord deliver us from falling into that state of soul in which crosses are of no benefit to us! God loves a cheerful giver, according to Saint Paul. (See 2 Corinthians 9:7.) Ah, what must be His love for those who, in a cheerful and absolute abandonment, resign themselves to the entire extent of His crucifying will!

Letter 3:
The Beauty of the Cross

I cannot but wonder at the virtue that lies in suffering; we are worth nothing without the cross. I tremble and am in an agony while it lasts, and all my conviction of its salutary effects vanish under the torture, but when it is over, I look back at it with admiration and am ashamed that I bore it so ill. This experience of my folly is a deep lesson of wisdom to me.

Whatever may be the state of your sick friend and whatever the issue of her disease, she is blessed in being so quiet under the hand of God. If she dies, she dies to the Lord; if she lives, she lives to Him. "Either the cross or death," says Saint Teresa.

Nothing is beyond the necessity of the cross but the established kingdom of God; when we bear it in love, it is His kingdom begun, with which we must remain satisfied while it is His pleasure. You have need of the cross, as well as I do. The faithful Giver of every good gift distributes them to each of us with His own hand, blessed be His name! Ah, how good it is to be chastened for our profit!

Letter 4: The Death of Self

I cannot express to you, my dear sister, how deeply I sympathize with your afflictions, but my grief is not unmixed with consolation. God loves you since He does not spare you, but lays upon you the cross of Jesus Christ. Whatever light, whatever feeling we may possess, is all a delusion if it leads us not to the real and constant practice of dying to self. We cannot die without suffering; neither can we be said to be dead while there is still any part in us that is alive. That death with which God blesses the soul pierces even to the dividing asunder of soul and spirit and of the joints and marrow. He who sees in us what we cannot see knows full well where the blow should fall. He takes away that which we are most reluctant to give up. Pain is only felt where there is life, and where there is life is just the place where death is needed. Our Father wastes no time by cutting into parts that are already dead; if He sought to continue life, He would do so, but He seeks to destroy, and this He can only accomplish by cutting into that which is quick and living. You need not expect Him to attack those gross and wicked desires that you renounced forever when you gave yourself away to Him, but He will prove you, perhaps, by destroying your liberty of soul and by depriving you of your most spiritual consolations.

Would you resist? Ah, no! Suffer all things! This death must be voluntary and can only be accomplished to that extent to which you are willing it should be. To resist death and repel its advances is not being willing to die. Give up voluntarily, then, to the good pleasure of God, all your reliance, even the most spiritual, whenever He may seem disposed to take them from you. What fear you, O you of little faith? Do you fear that He may not be able to supply to you from Himself that succor that He takes away on the part of man? And why does He take it away except to supply it from Himself and to purify you by the painful lesson? I see that every way is shut up and that God means to accomplish His work in you by cutting off every human resource. He is a jealous God; He is not willing you should owe what He is about to perform in you to any other than to Himself alone.

Give yourself up to His plans; be led wherever He wills by His providences. Beware how you seek aid from man when God forbids it; they can only give you what He gives them for you. Why should you be troubled that you can no longer drink from the aqueduct when you are led to the perennial spring itself from which its waters are derived?

Letter 5: Peace Lies in Simplicity and Obedience

Cultivate peace; be deaf to your too prolific imagination. Its great activity not only injures the health of your body but introduces aridity into your soul. You consume yourself to no purpose;

peace and interior sweetness are destroyed by your restlessness. Do you think God can speak in those soft and tender accents that melt the soul in the midst of such a tumult as you excite by your incessant hurry of thought? Be quiet, and He will soon be heard. Indulge but a single scruple—to be scrupulously obedient.

You ask for consolation, but you do not perceive that you have been led to the brink of the fountain and refuse to drink. Peace and consolation are to be found only in simple obedience. Be faithful in obeying without reference to your scruples, and you will soon find that the rivers of living water will flow according to the promise. You will receive according to the measure of your faith—*much* if you believe much, *nothing* if you believe nothing and continue to give ear to your empty imaginations.

You dishonor true love by the supposition that it is anxious about such trifles as continually occupy your attention; it goes straight to God in pure simplicity. Satan is transformed into an Angel of Light; he assumes the beautiful form of a scrupulous love and a tender conscience, but you should know by experience the trouble and danger into which he will lead you by vehement scruples. Everything depends upon your faithfulness in repelling his first advances.

If you become ingenuous and simple in your desires, I think you will have been more pleasing to God than if you had suffered a hundred martyrdoms. Turn all your anxieties toward your delay in offering a sacrifice so right in the sight of God. Can true love hesitate when it is required to please its well beloved?

Letter 6:
The True Source of Peace Is in the Surrender of the Will

Remain in peace; the fervor of devotion does not depend upon you. All that lies in your power is the direction of your will. Give that up to God without reservation. The important question is not how much you enjoy religion but whether you will whatever God wills. Humbly confess your faults; be detached from the world and abandoned to God. Love Him more than yourself and His glory more than your life; the least you can do is to desire and ask for such a love. God will then love you and put His peace in your heart.

LETTER 7: TRUE GOOD IS REACHED ONLY BY ABANDONMENT

Evil is changed into good when it is received in patience through the love of God, while good is changed into evil when we become attached to it through the love of self. True good lies only in detachment and abandonment to God. You are now in the trial; put yourself confidently and without reserve into His hand. What would I not sacrifice to see you once more restored in body but heartily sick of the love of the world! Attachment to ourselves is a thousand times more infectious than a contagious poison, for it contains the venom of self. I pray for you with all my heart.

LETTER 8: KNOWLEDGE PUFFS UP; CHARITY EDIFIES

I am happy to hear of your frame of mind and to find you communicating in simplicity everything that takes place within you. Never hesitate to write me whatever you think God requires.

It is not at all surprising that you have a sort of jealous ambition to advance in the spiritual life and to be intimate with persons of distinction who are pious. Such things are by nature very flattering to our self-love, and it eagerly seeks them. But we should not strive to gratify such an ambition by making great progress in the religious life and by cultivating the acquaintance of persons high in honor; our aim should be to die to the flattering delights of self-love by becoming humble and in love with obscurity and contempt and having a single eye to God.

We may hear about perfection without end and become perfectly familiar with its language, yet be as far from its attainment as ever. Our great aim should be to be deaf to ourselves, to listen to God in silence, to renounce every vanity, and to devote ourselves to solid virtue. Let us speak but little and do much without a thought as to whether we are observed or not.

God will teach you more than the most experienced Christians and better than all the books that the world has ever seen. And what is your object in such an eager chase after knowledge? Are you not aware that all we need is to be poor in spirit and to know nothing but Christ and Him crucified? Knowledge puffs up; it is only charity that can edify. (See 1 Corinthians 8:1.) Be content with charity, then, alone. What? Is it possible that the love of God and the abandonment of self for His sake are only to be reached through the acquisition of so much knowledge? You have already more than you use and need further illuminations much less than the practice of what you already know. O how deceived we are when we suppose we are advancing because our vain curiosity is gratified by the enlightenment of our intellect! Be humble, and expect not the gifts of God from man.

Letter 9:
Not Choosing the Manner in Which Our Blessings Are Bestowed

You know what God requires of you; will you refuse? You perceive that your resistance to the drawings of His grace arises solely from self-love. Will you allow the refinements of pride and the most ingenious inventions of self to reject the mercies of God? You who have so many scruples in relation to the passing thought, which is involuntary and therefore innocent, who confess so many things that should rather be dismissed at once, have you no scruples about your long-continued resistance to the Holy Spirit because He has not seen fit to confer the benefits you desire by a channel that was flattering to your self-love?

What matter if you received the gifts of grace as beggars receive bread? The gifts themselves would be neither less pure nor less precious. Your heart would only be the more worthy of God if, by its humility and annihilation, it attracted the relief that He was disposed to send. Is this the way you put off self? Is this the view that pure faith takes of the instrument of God? Is it thus that you die to the life of self within? To what purpose are your readings about pure love and your frequent devotions? How can you read what condemns the very depths of your soul? You are influenced not only by self-interest but by the persuasions of pride when you reject the gifts of God because they do not come in a shape to suit your taste. How can you pray? What is the language of God in the depths of your soul? He asks nothing but death, and you desire nothing but life. How can you put up to Him a prayer for His grace with a restriction that He must send it only by a channel demanding no sacrifice on your part but ministering to the gratification of your carnal pride?

Letter 10: The Discovery and Death of Self

Yes! I joyfully consent that you call me your father! I am so and will be always; there needs only on your part a full and confident persuasion of it, which will come when your heart is enlarged. Self-love now shuts it up. We are in a strait place, indeed, when we are enclosed in self, but when we emerge from that prison and enter into the immensity of God and the liberty of His children, we are set at large.

I am rejoiced to find that God has reduced you to a state of weakness. Your self-love can neither be convinced nor vanquished by any other means, ever finding secret resources and impenetrable retreats in your courage and ingenuity. It was hidden from your eyes while it fed upon the subtle poison of an apparent generosity, by which you constantly sacrificed yourself for others. God has forced it to cry aloud, to come forth into open day, and to display its excessive jealousy. O how painful, but how useful, are these seasons of weakness? While any self-love remains, we are afraid of its being revealed, but so long as the least symptom of it lurks in the most secret recesses of the heart, God pursues it, and by some infinitely merciful blow, forces it into the light. The poison then becomes the remedy; self-love, pushed to extremity, discovers itself in all its deformity by a transport of despair, and it disgraces all the refinements and dissipates the flattering illusions of a whole life. God sets before your eyes your idol—self. You behold it and cannot turn your eyes away, and as you have no longer power over yourself, you cannot keep the sight from others.

Thus to exhibit self-love without its mask is the most mortifying punishment that can be inflicted. We no longer behold it wise, discreet, polite, self-possessed, and courageous in sacrificing itself for others; it is no longer the self-love whose nourishment consisted in the belief that it had need of nothing and the persuasion that its greatness and generosity deserved a different name. It is the selfishness of a silly child screaming at the loss of an apple; but it is far more tormenting, for it also weeps from rage that it has wept. It cannot be still and refuses all comfort, because its venomous character has been detected. It beholds itself foolish, rude, and impertinent, and is forced to look its own frightful countenance in the face. It says with Job, "*For the thing which I greatly feared is come upon me, and that which I was afraid of is come unto me*" (Job 3:25). For precisely that which it most fears is the most necessary means of its destruction.

We have no need that God should attack in us what has neither life nor sensibility. It is the living only that must die, and all the rest is nothing. This, then, is what you needed, to behold a self-love convinced, sensitive, gross, and palpable. And now all you have to do is to be quietly willing to look at it as it is; the moment you can do this, it will have disappeared.

You ask for a remedy that you may get well. You do not need to be cured but to be slain; seek not impatiently for a remedy, but let death come. Be careful, however, lest a certain courageous resolve to avail yourself of no remedy be itself a remedy in disguise and give aid and comfort to this cursed life. Seek no consolation for self-love, and do not conceal the disease. Reveal everything in simplicity and holiness, and then suffer yourself to die.

But this is not to be accomplished by any exertion of strength. Weakness has become your only possession; all strength is out of place. It only serves to render the agony longer and more distressing. If you expire from exhaustion, you will die so much the quicker and less violently. A dying life must of necessity be painful. Cordials are a cruelty to the sufferer on the wheel; he longs only for the fatal blow, not food or sustenance. If it was possible to weaken him and hasten his death, we should abridge his sufferings, but we can do nothing. The hand alone that tied him to his torture can deliver him from the remains of suffering life.

Ask, then, for neither remedies, sustenance, nor death. To ask for death is impatience; to ask food or remedies is to prolong our agony. What, then, should we do? Let alone; seek nothing and hold on to nothing. Confess everything, not as a means of consolation, but through humility and desire to yield. Look to me not as a source of life but as a means of death. As an instrument of life would belie its purpose if it did not minister to life, so an instrument of death would be falsely named, if, in lieu of slaying, it kept alive. Let me, then, be (or at least seem to you to be) hard, unfeeling, indifferent, pitiless, wearied, annoyed, and contemptuous. God knows how far it is from the truth, but He permits it all to appear, and I will be much more serviceable to you in this false and imaginary character than by my affection and real assistance, for the point is not how you are to be sustained and kept alive, but how you are to lose all and die.

Letter 11:
The Sight of Our Imperfections Should Not Take Away Our Peace

There is something very hidden and very deceptive in your suffering, for while you seem to yourself to be wholly occupied with the glory of God, in your inmost soul it is self alone that occasions all your trouble. You are, indeed, desirous that God should be glorified, but that it should take place by means of your perfection, and you thus cherish the sentiments of self-love. It is simply a refined pretext for dwelling in self. If you would truly derive profit from the discovery of your imperfections, neither justify nor condemn on their account, but quietly lay them before God, conforming your will to His in all things that you cannot understand, and remaining at peace, for peace is the order of God for every condition whatever. There is, in fact, a peace of conscience that sinners themselves should enjoy when awakened to repentance. Their suffering should be peaceful and mingled with consolation. Remember the beautiful word that once delighted you, that the Lord was not in noise and confusion, but in the still, small voice. (See 1 Kings 19:11–12.)

Letter 12: Living by the Cross and by Faith

Everything is a cross; I have no joy but bitterness; but the heaviest cross must be borne in peace. At times, it can neither be borne nor dragged; we can only fall down beneath it, overwhelmed and exhausted. I pray that God may spare you as much as possible in apportioning your suffering. It is our daily bread; God alone knows how much we need, and we must live in faith upon the means of death, confident, though we see it not, that God, with secret compassion, proportions our trials to the unperceived relief that He administers within. This life of faith is the most penetrating of all deaths.

Letter 13: Despair at Our Imperfection Is a Greater Obstacle than the Imperfection Itself

Be not concerned about your defects. Love without ceasing, and you will be much forgiven, because you have loved much. (See Luke 7:47.) We are apt to seek the delights and selfish supports of love rather than love itself. We deceive ourselves even in supposing we are endeavoring to love when we are only trying to see that we love. We are more occupied with the love, says Saint Francis of Sales, than with the well beloved. If He were our only object, we should be all taken up with Him; but when we are employed in obtaining an assurance of His love, we are still in a measure busy with self.

Our defects, regarded in peace and in the spirit of love, are instantly consumed by love itself, but considered in the light of self, they make us restless and interrupt the presence of God and the exercise of perfect love. The chagrin we feel at our own defects is ordinarily a greater fault than the original defect itself. You are wholly taken up with the less of the two faults, like a person whom I have just seen, who, after reading about the life of one of the saints, was so enraged at his own comparative imperfection that he entirely abandoned the idea of living a devoted life. I judge of your fidelity by your peace and liberty of soul; the more peaceful and enlarged your heart, the nearer you seem to be to God.

Letter 14:
Pure Faith Sees God Alone

Be not anxious about the future; it is opposed to grace. When God sends you consolation, regard Him only in it, enjoy it day by day as the Israelites received their manna, and do not endeavor to lay it up in store. There are two peculiarities of pure faith: it sees God alone under all the imperfect envelopes that conceal Him,[4] and it holds the soul incessantly in suspense. We are kept constantly in the air without being suffered to touch a foot to solid ground. The comfort of the present instant will be wholly inappropriate to the next; we must let God act with the most perfect freedom in whatever belongs to Him and think only of being faithful in all that depends upon ourselves. This momentary dependence, this darkness and this peace of the soul under the utter uncertainty of the future, is a true martyrdom that takes place silently and without any stir. It is death by a slow fire, and the end comes so imperceptibly and interiorly that it is often almost as much hidden

4. Note from the editor: Pure faith cannot see the neighbor that succeeds (as he blindly thinks) in injuring us nor the disease that attacks our bodies. That would be to stay its eye upon the glass, in which it would see a thousand flaws and imperfections that would annoy it and destroy its peace. It looks right through and discovers God, and what He permits, it cannot but joyfully acquiesce in. "The man that looks on glass, / On it may stay his eye; / Or if he pleaseth, through it pass, / And then the heaven espy." —George Herbert

from the sufferer himself as from those who are unacquainted with his state. When God removes His gifts from you, He knows how and when to replace them, either by others or by Himself. He can raise up children from the very stones.

Eat then your daily bread without thought for the morrow. "*Sufficient unto the day is the evil thereof*" (Matthew 6:34). Tomorrow will take thought for the things of itself. The one who feeds you today is the same one you will look to for food tomorrow; manna will fall again from heaven in the midst of the desert before the children of God will want any good thing.

Letter 15:
Our Knowledge Stands in the Way of Our Becoming Wise

Live in peace, my dear young lady, without any thought for the future; perhaps there will be none for you. You have no present, even, of your own, for you must use it only in accordance with the designs of God, to whom it truly belongs. Continue the good works that occupy you, since you have an attraction that way and can readily accomplish them. Avoid distractions and the consequences of your excessive vivacity, and above all things, be faithful to the present moment, and you will receive all necessary grace.

It is not enough to be detached from the world; we must become lowly also. In detachment, we renounce the things without; in lowliness, we abandon self. Every shadow of perceptible pride must be left behind, and the pride of wisdom and virtue is more dangerous than that of worldly fortune, as it has a show of right and is more refined.

We must be lowly minded in all points and appropriate nothing to ourselves, our virtue and courage least of all. You rest too much in your own courage, disinterestedness, and uprightness. The babe owns nothing; it treats a diamond and an apple alike. Be a babe; have nothing of your own. Forget yourself, give way on all occasions, and let the smallest be greater than you.

Pray simply from the heart, from pure love, and not from the head, from the intellect alone.

Your true instruction is to be found in spoliation; deep recollection; silence of the whole soul before God; renouncement of your own spirit; and in the love of lowliness, obscurity, feebleness, and annihilation. This ignorance is the accomplished teacher of all truth; knowledge cannot attain to it or can reach it but superficially.

Letter 16: Loving and Welcoming Those Who Injure Us

I sympathize with you, as I ought, in all your troubles, but I can do nothing else except pray God that He would console you. You have great need of the gift of His Spirit to sustain you in your difficulties and to restrain your natural vivacity under the trials that are so fitted to excite it. As to the letter touching your birth, I think you should lay it before God alone and beg His mercy upon him who has sought to injure you.

I have always perceived, or thought that I have perceived, that you were sensitive on that point. God always attacks us on our weak side. We do not aim to kill a person by striking a blow at his insensible parts, such as the hair or nails, but by endeavoring to reach at once the noble organs, the immediate seats of life. When God would have us die to self, He always touches the tenderest spot, that which is fullest of life. It is thus that He distributes crosses. Suffer yourself to be humbled. Silence and peace under humiliation are the true good of the soul; we are tempted under a thousand specious pretexts to speak humbly, but it is far better to be humbly silent. The humility that can yet talk has need of careful watching; self-love derives comfort from its outward words.

Do not suffer yourself to get excited by what is said about you. Let the world talk. Do you strive to do the will of God? As for that of men, you could never succeed in doing it to their satisfaction, and it is not worth the pains. A moment of silence, of peace, and of union to God will amply recompense you for every calumny that will be uttered against you. We must love our fellows without expecting friendship from them. They leave us and return; they go and come. Let them do as they will; it is but a feather, the sport of the wind. See God only in them; it is He who afflicts or consoles us, by means of them, according as we have need.

Letter 17:
Quietness in God, Our True Resource

Warmth of imagination, ardor of feeling, acuteness of reasoning, and fluency of expression can do but little. The true agent is a perfect abandonment before God in which we do everything by the light that He gives and are content with the success that He bestows. This continual death is a blessed life known to few. A single word, uttered from this rest, will do more, even in outward affairs, than all our most eager and officious care. It is the Spirit of God who then speaks the word, and it loses none of its force and authority but enlightens, persuades, moves, and edifies. We have accomplished everything and have scarce said anything.

On the other hand, if left to the excitability of our natural temperament, we talk forever, indulging in a thousand subtle and superfluous reflections. We are constantly afraid of not saying or doing enough. We get angry, excited, exhausted, distracted, and finally make no headway. Your disposition has an especial need of these maxims; they are as necessary for your body as for your soul, and your physician and your spiritual adviser should act together.

Let the water flow beneath the bridge; let men be men—that is to say, weak, vain, inconstant, unjust, false, and presumptuous. Let the world be the world still; you cannot prevent it. Let everyone follow his own inclination and habits. You cannot recast them, and the best course is to let them be as they are and bear with them. Do not think it strange when you witness unreasonableness and injustice; rest in peace in the bosom of God. He sees it all more clearly than you do and yet permits it. Be content to do quietly and gently what it becomes you to do, and let everything else be to you as though it was not.

Letter 18: True Friendships Are Founded Only in God

We must be content with what God gives without having any choice of our own. It is right that His will should be done, not ours, and that His should become ours without the least reservation in order that it may be done on earth as it is done in heaven. This is a hundred times more valuable an attainment than to be engaged in the view or consolation of self.

O how near we are to each other when we are all united in God! How well we converse when we have but a single will and a single thought in Him who is all things in us! Would you find your true friends, then? Seek them only in Him who is the single source of true and eternal friendship. Would you speak with or hear from them? Sink in silence into the bosom of Him who is the word, the life, and the soul of all those who speak and live the truth. You will find in Him not only every want supplied but everything perfect that you find so imperfect in the creatures in whom you confide.

Letter 19: The Cross a Source of Our Pleasure

I sympathize with all your distresses, but we must carry the cross with Christ in this transitory life. We will soon have no time to suffer; we will reign with God our consolation, who will have wiped away our tears with His own hand and from before whose presence pain and sighing will forever flee away. While this fleeting moment of trial is permitted us, let us not lose the slightest portion of the worth of the cross. Let us suffer in humility and in peace; our self-love exaggerates our distresses and magnifies them in our imagination. A cross borne in simplicity, without the interference of self-love to augment it, is only half a cross. Suffering in this simplicity of love, we are not only happy in spite of the cross, but because of it, for love is pleased in suffering for the well beloved, and the cross that forms us into His image is a consoling bond of love.

Letter 20: The Absence of Feeling and the Revelation of Self

I pray God that this New Year may be full of grace and blessing to you. I am not surprised that you do not enjoy recollection as you did on being delivered from a long and painful agitation. Everything is liable to be exhausted. A lively disposition, accustomed to active exertion, soon languishes in solitude and inaction. For a great number of years, you have been necessarily much distracted by external activity, and it was this circumstance that made me fear the effect of the life of abandonment upon you. You were at first in the fervor of your beginnings, when no difficulties appear formidable. You said with Peter, "*It is good for us to be here*" (Matthew 17:4; Mark 9:5; Luke 9:33), but it is often with us as it was with him, that we know not what we say see Mark 9:6). In our moments of enjoyment, we feel as if we could do everything; in the time of temptation and discouragement, we think we can do nothing and believe that all is lost. But we are alike deceived in both.

You should not be disturbed at any distraction that you may experience; the causes of it lay concealed within, even when you felt such zeal for recollection. Your temperament and habits all conduce to making you active and eager. It was only weariness and exhaustion that caused you to relish an opposite life. But by fidelity to grace, you will gradually become permanently introduced into the experience of which you have had a momentary taste. God bestowed it that you might see whether He would lead you; He then takes it away so that we may be made sensible that it does not belong to us, that we are neither able to procure it nor preserve it, and that it is a gift of grace that must be asked in all humility.

Be not amazed at finding yourself sensitive, impatient, haughty, self-willed; you must be made to perceive that such is your natural disposition. We must bear the yoke of the daily confusion of our sins, says Saint Augustine. We must be made to feel our weakness, our wretchedness, our inability to correct ourselves. We must despair of our own heart and have no hope but in God. We must bear with ourselves, without flattering and without neglecting a single effort for our correction. We must be instructed as to our true character while waiting for God's time to take it away.

Let us become lowly under His all-powerful hand; yielding and manageable as often as we perceive any resistance in our will. Be silent as much as you can. Be in no haste to judge; suspend your decisions, your likes and dislikes. Stop at once when you become aware that your activity is hurried, and do not be too eager even for good things.

Letter 21: The Imperfection of Others to Be Borne in Love

It is a long while since I renewed the assurance of my attachment to you in our Lord. It is, nevertheless, greater than ever. I desire with all my heart that you may always find in your household the peace and consolation that you enjoyed in the beginning. To be content with even the best of people, we must be content with little and bear a great deal. Those who are most perfect have many imperfections, and we have great faults, so that between the two, mutual toleration becomes very difficult. We must bear one another's burdens and so fulfill the law of Christ (see Galatians 6:2), thus setting off one against the other in love. Peace and unanimity will be much aided by frequent silence, habitual recollection, prayer, self-abandonment, renunciation of all vain criticisms, and a faithful departure from the vain reflections of a jealous and difficult self-love. This simplicity would put an end to much trouble! Happy is he who neither listens to self nor to the tales of others!

Be content with leading a simple life according to your condition. Be obedient and bear your daily cross; you need it, and it is bestowed by the pure mercy of God. The grand point is to despise self from the heart and to be willing to be despised, if God permits it. Feed upon Him alone. Saint Augustine says that his mother lived upon prayer. Do you do so likewise and die to everything else? We can only live to God by the continual death of self.

Letter 22: The Fear of Death Is Taken Away by the Grace of God

I am not in the least surprised to learn that your impression of death becomes more lively as age and infirmity bring it nearer. I experience the same thing. There is an age at which death is forced upon our consideration more frequently, by more irresistible reflections, and by a time of retirement in which we have fewer distractions. God makes use of this rough trial to undeceive us in respect to our courage, to make us feel our weakness, and to keep us in all humility in His own hands.

Nothing is more humiliating than a troubled imagination in which we search in vain for our former confidence in God. This is the crucible of humiliation in which the heart is purified by a sense of its weakness and unworthiness. In His sight, no living man will be justified (see Psalm 143:2); yes, the heavens are not clean in His sight (see Job 15:15), and in many things, we offend all (see James 3:2). We behold our faults and not our virtues, the latter of which it would be even dangerous to behold if they are real.

We must go straight on through this deprivation without interruption, just as we were endeavoring to walk in the way of God before being disturbed. If we should perceive any fault that needs correction, we must be faithful to the light given us, but do it carefully, lest we be led into false scruples. We must then remain at peace, not listening to the voice of self-love, mourning over our approaching death, but detaching ourselves from life, offering it in sacrifice to God, and confidently abandoning ourselves to Him. Saint Ambrose was asked, when dying, whether he was afraid of the judgments of God; "We have a good Master," said he, and so must we reply to ourselves. We need to die in the most impenetrable uncertainty, not only as to God's judgment upon us but as to our own characters. We must, as Saint Augustine has it, be so reduced as to have nothing to present before God but *our wretchedness* and *His mercy*. Our wretchedness is the proper object of His mercy, and His mercy is all our merit. In your hours of sadness, read whatever will strengthen your confidence and establish your heart. "*Truly God is good to Israel, even to such as are of a clean heart*" (Psalm 73:1). Pray for this cleanness of heart, which is so pleasing in His sight and which renders Him so compassionate to our failings.

LETTER 23:
SENSITIVENESS UNDER REPROOF THE SUREST SIGN WE NEEDED IT

I greatly desire that you may have interior peace. You know that it cannot be found except in lowliness of mind, and lowliness is not real, except when it is produced by God upon every proper occasion. These occasions are chiefly when we are blamed by someone who disapproves of us and when we experience inward weakness. We must accustom ourselves to bearing both these trials.

We are truly lowly when we are no longer taken by surprise at finding ourselves corrected from without and incorrigible within. We are then like little children, below everything, and are willing to be so; we feel that our reprovers are right but that we are unable to overcome ourselves in order to correct our faults. Then we despair of ourselves and expect nothing except from God; the reproofs of others, harsh and unfeeling as they may be, seem to us less than we deserve. If we cannot bear them, we condemn our sensitiveness more than all our other imperfections. Correction cannot then make us more humble than it finds us. The interior rebellion, far from hindering the profit of the correction, convinces us of its absolute necessity. In truth, the reproof would not have been felt if it had not cut into some living part; had death been there, we should not have perceived it. And thus, the more acutely we feel, the more certainly we know that the correction was necessary.

I beg your forgiveness if I have said anything too harsh, but do not doubt my affection for you, and count as nothing everything that comes from me. See only the hand of God, which makes use of the awkwardness of mine to deal you a painful blow. The pain proves that I have touched a sore spot. Yield to God, acquiesce in all His dealings, and you will soon be at rest and in harmony within. You know well enough how to give this advice to others; the occasion is important, even critical. O what grace will descend upon you if you will bear, like a little child, all the means God employs to humiliate and dispossess you of your senses and will! I pray that He may so diminish you, so that you can no longer be found at all.

Letter 24: Imperfection Only Is Intolerant of Imperfection

It has seemed to me that you have need of more largeness of heart in relation to the defects of others. I know that you cannot help seeing them when they come before you, nor prevent the opinions you involuntarily form concerning the motives of some of those about you. You cannot even get rid of a certain degree of trouble that these things cause you. It will be enough if you are willing to bear with those defects that are unmistakable, refrain from condemning those that are doubtful, and not suffer yourself to be so afflicted by them as to cause a coolness of feeling between you and the other person.

Perfection is easily tolerant of the imperfections of others; it becomes all things to all men. We must not be surprised at the greatest defects in good souls and must quietly leave them alone until God gives the signal of gradual removal; otherwise, we will pull up the wheat with the tares. God leaves, in the most advanced souls, certain weaknesses entirely disproportioned to their eminent state. As workmen, in excavating the soil from a field, leave certain pillars of earth that indicate the original level of the surface and serve to measure the amount of material removed—God, in the same way, leaves pillars of testimony to the extent of His work in the most pious souls.

Such persons must labor, each one in his degree, for his own correction, and you must labor to bear with their weaknesses. You know from experience the bitterness of the work of correction; strive, then, to find means to make it less bitter to others. You have not an eager zeal to correct, but a sensitiveness that easily shuts up your heart.

I pray you more than ever not to spare my faults. If you should think you see one that is not really there, there is no harm done. If I find that your counsel wounds me, my sensitiveness demonstrates that you have discovered a sore spot, but if not, you will have done me an excellent kindness in exercising my humility and accustoming me to reproof. I ought to be more lowly than others as I am higher in position, and God demands of me a more absolute death to everything. I need this simplicity, and I trust it will be the means of cementing rather than of weakening our attachment.

Letter 25: We Should Listen to God and Not to Self-love

I beseech you not to listen to yourself. Self-love whispers in one ear and the love of God in the other. The first is restless, bold, eager, and impetuous; the other is simple, peaceful, and speaks but a few words in a mild and gentle voice. The moment we attend to the voice of self, crying in our ears, we can no longer hear the modest tones of holy love. Each speaks only of its single object. Self-love entertains us with self, which, according to it, is never sufficiently well attended to; it talks of friendship, regard, esteem, and is in despair at everything but flattery. The love of God, on the other hand, desires that self should be forgotten, that it should be trodden under foot and broken as an idol, and that God should become the self of espoused souls and occupy them as others are occupied by self. Let the vain, complaining babbler—self-love—be silenced, so that in the stillness of the heart, we may listen to that other love that speaks only when addressed.

Letter 26: Absolute Trust, the Shortest Road to God

I have no doubt that God constantly treats you as one of His friends, that is, with crosses, sufferings, and humiliations. The ways and means of God by which He draws souls to Himself accomplishes His design much more rapidly and effectually than all the efforts of the creature, for they destroy self-love at its very root, where, with all our pains, we could scarce discover it. God knows all its windings and attacks it in its strongest holds.

If we had strength and faith enough to trust ourselves entirely to God and follow Him wherever He should lead us, we should have no need of any great effort of mind to reach perfection. But as we are so weak in faith as to require to know all the way without trusting in God, our road is lengthened, and our spiritual affairs get behind. Abandon yourself to God as absolutely as possible, and continue to do so till your latest breath, and He will never desert you.

Letter 27: The Time of Temptation and Distress Is No Time to Form Resolves

Your excessive distress is like a summer torrent that must be suffered to run away. Nothing makes any impression upon you, and you think you have the most substantial evidence for the most imaginary states; it is the ordinary result of great suffering. God permits you, notwithstanding your excellent faculties, to be blind to what lies immediately before you and to think you see clearly what does not exist at all. God will be glorified in your heart if you will be faithful in yielding to His designs. But nothing would be more injudicious than the forming of resolutions in a state of distress, which is manifestly accompanied by an inability to do anything according to God.

When you have become calm, then do in a spirit of recollection what you will perceive to be nearest the will of God respecting you. Return gradually to devotion, simplicity, and the oblivion of self. Commune with and listen to God, and be deaf to self. Then do all that is in your heart; for I have no fear that a spirit of that sort will permit you to take any wrong step. But to suppose that we are sane when we are in the very agony of distress and under the influence of a violent temptation of self-love is to ensure our being led astray. Ask any experienced adviser, and he will tell you that you are to make no resolutions until you have re-entered into peace and recollection. You will learn from him that the readiest way to self-deception is to trust in ourselves in a state of suffering, in which nature is so unreasonable and irritated.

You will say that I desire to prevent you doing as you ought if I forbid your doing it at the only moment when you are capable of it. God forbid! I neither desire to permit nor hinder; my only wish is so to advise you that you will not be found wanting toward God. Now it is as clear as day that you would fail in that respect if you took counsel at the hands of a self-love wounded to the quick and an irritation verging upon despair. Would you change anything to gratify your self-love when God does not desire it? God forbid! Wait, then, until you will be in a condition to be advised. To enjoy the true advantages of illumination, we must be equally ready for every alternative, and must have nothing that we are not cheerfully disposed at once to sacrifice for His sake.

Letter 28: Who Has Love, Has All

Since yesterday, I have thought frequently on the matters you have communicated to me, and I have increasing confidence that God will sustain you. Though you take no great pleasure in religious exercises, you must not neglect to be faithful in them, as far as your health will permit. A convalescent has but little appetite, but he must eat to sustain life.

It would be very serviceable to you if you could occasionally have a few minutes of Christian converse with such of your family as you can confide in, and as to the choice, be guided in perfect liberty by your impressions at the moment. God does not call you by any lively emotions, and I heartily rejoice at it, if you will but remain faithful, for a fidelity unsustained by delights is far purer and safer from danger than one accompanied by those tender feelings, which may be seated too exclusively in the imagination. A little reading and recollection every day will be the means of insensibly giving you light and strength for all the sacrifices God will require of you. Love Him, and I will acquit you of everything else, for everything else will come by love. I do not ask from you a love tender and emotional, but only that your will should lean toward love and that, notwithstanding all the corrupt desires of your heart, you should prefer God before self and the whole world.

Letter 29: Weakness Preferable to Strength; Practice Better than Knowledge

I am told, my dear child in our Lord, that you are suffering from sickness. I suffer with you, for I love you dearly, but I cannot but kiss the hand that smites you, and I pray you to kiss it lovingly with me. You have, up to this time, abused your health and the pleasures derived from it; this weakness and its attendant pains are the natural consequence of such a course.

I pray God that He may depress your spirit even more than your body, and while He comforts the latter according to your need, that He may entirely vanquish the former. O how strong we are when we begin to perceive that we are but weakness and infirmity! Then we are ever ready to believe that we are mistaken and to correct ourselves while confessing it. Our minds are ever open to the illumination of others. Then we are authoritative in nothing and say the most decided things with simplicity and deference for others. Then we do not object to be judged, and we submit without hesitation to the censure of the first comer. At the same time, we judge no one without absolute necessity; we speak only to those who desire it, mentioning the imperfections we seem to have discovered without dogmatism, and rather to gratify their wishes than from a desire to be believed or create a reputation for wisdom.

I pray God that He may keep you faithful to His grace and that He who has begun a good work in you will perform it until the day of Jesus Christ. (See Philippians 1:6.) We must bear with ourselves with patience and without flattery, and remain in unceasing subjection to every means of overcoming our thoughts and inward repugnance; we will thus become more pliable to the impressions of grace in the practice of the gospel. But let this work be done quietly and peacefully, and let it not be entered upon too eagerly, as though it could all be accomplished in a single day. Let us *reason* little but *do* much. If we are not careful, the acquisition of knowledge will so occupy this life that we will need another to reduce our acquirements into practice. We are in danger of believing ourselves advanced toward perfection in proportion to our knowledge of the way. But all our beautiful theories, far from assisting in the death of self, only serve to nourish the life of Adam in us by a secret delight and confidence in our illumination.[5] Be quit then of all trust in your own power and in your own knowledge of the way, and you will make a great stride toward perfection. Humility and self-distrust, with a frank ingenuousness, are fundamental virtues for you.

---

5. Note from the editor: This seems one of the most common as well as most serious mistakes to which spiritual persons are liable. God gives the knowledge and desires to us to put it in practice, but the moment we see it, we are so carried away with delight that we forget that there is anything else to be done; whereas we have comparatively slender reason to rejoice until it is put in vital operation in the life. You see, says the Savior, but do not perceive; you hear, but do not understand. (See Matthew 13:13.) Food, lying undigested in the stomach, is not only of no service to the body, but, if not removed, will become a serious injury. It is only when it is assimilated and mingled with the blood, and when it appears by its good effects in our hands, feet, head, and trunk, that it can be said to have become our own. To have a divine truth in the intellect is indeed a matter of thanksgiving, but it will avail only to our condemnation if it is not also loved in the heart and acted out in the life. Let us remember that it is not the knowledge of the way that God desires in us but the practice of it—not light, but love. For though I understand all mysteries and all knowledge, and have not charity, I am nothing. (See 1 Corinthians 13:2.)

Letter 30: The True Guide to Knowledge

Your mind is too much occupied with exterior things and (still worse) with argumentation to be able to act with a frequent thought of God. I am always afraid of your excessive inclination to reason; it is a hindrance to that recollection and silence in which God reveals Himself. Be humble, simple, and sincerely abstracted with men; be recollected, calm, and devoid of reasoning before God. The persons who have up to this time had most influence with you have been infinitely dry, reasoning, critical, and opposed to a true inner life. However little you might listen to them, you would hear only endless reasoning and a dangerous curiosity that would insensibly draw you out of grace and plunge you into the depths of nature. Habits of long-standing are easily revived, and the changes that cause us to revert to our original position are less easily perceived because they are natural to our constitution. Distrust them, then, and beware of beginnings that, in fact, include the end.

It has now been four months since I have had any leisure for study, but I am very happy to forego study and to not cling to anything when Providence would take it away. It may be that during the coming winter, I will have leisure for my library; but I will enter it then, keeping one foot on the threshold, ready to leave it at the slightest intimation. The mind must fast as well as the body. I have no desire to write or to speak or to be spoken about or to reason or to persuade any. I live every day aridly enough and with certain exterior inconveniences that beset me; but I amuse myself whenever I have an opportunity, if I need recreation. Those who make almanacs upon me and are afraid of me are sadly deceived. God bless them! I am far from being so foolish as to incommode myself for the sake of annoying them. I would say to them as Abraham said to Lot: "*Is not the whole land before thee?*" (Genesis 13:9). If you go to the east, I will go to the west.

Happy is he who is indeed free! The Son of God alone can make us free, but He can do it only by snapping every bond. And how is this to be done? By that sword that divides husband and wife, father and son, brother and sister. The world is then no longer of any account, but as long as it is anything to us, so long our freedom is but a word, and we are as easily captured as a bird whose leg is fastened by a thread. He seems to be free; the string is not visible, but he can only fly its length, and he is a prisoner. You see the moral. What I would have you possess is more valuable than all you are fearful of losing. Be faithful in what you know, so that you may be entrusted with more. Distrust your intellect, which has so often misled you. My own has been such a deceiver that I no longer count upon it. Be simple and firm in your simplicity. "*The fashion of this world passeth away*" (1 Corinthians 7:31). We will vanish with it if we make ourselves like it by reason of vanity, but the truth of God remains forever, and we will dwell with it if it alone occupies our attention.

Again I warn you, beware of philosophers and great reasoners. They will always be a snare to you and will do you more harm than you will know how to do them good. They linger and pine away in discussing exterior trifles and never reach the knowledge of the truth. Their curiosity is an insatiable spiritual avarice. They are as those conquerors who ravage the world without possessing it. Solomon, after a deep experience of it, testifies to the vanity of their researches.

We should never study but on an express intimation of Providence, and we should do it as we go to market, to buy the provision necessary for each day's needs. Then, too, we must study in the spirit of prayer. God is, at the same time, both truth and love. We can only know the truth in proportion to how much we love—when we love it, we understand it well. If we do not love love, we do not know love. He who loves much and remains humble and lowly in his ignorance is the well beloved one of the truth. He knows not only what philosophers are ignorant of, but what they do not desire to know. Would that you might obtain that knowledge that is reserved for babes and the simpleminded while it is hidden from the wise and prudent. (See Matthew 11:25.)

Letter 31:
The Channels That Bring God's Gifts

I am glad you find in the person of whom you speak the qualities you were in search of. God puts what He pleases where He pleases. Naaman could not be healed by all the waters of Syria, but had to go to those of Palestine. What does it matter from what quarter our light and help come? The source is the important point, not the conduit; that is the best channel that most exercises our faith, puts to shame our human wisdom, makes us simple and humble, and undeceives us in respect to our own power. Receive, then, whatever He bestows, in dependence upon the Spirit that blows where it chooses; we know not where it comes from or where it goes. (See John 3:8.) But we need not seek to know the secrets of God; let us only be obedient to what He reveals.

Too much reasoning is a great distraction. Those who reason—the indevout wise—quench the inward spirit, as the wind extinguishes a candle. After being with them for a while, we perceive our hearts dry and our minds off their center. Shun association with such men; they are full of danger to you.

There are some who appear recollected but whose appearance deceives us. It is easy to mistake a certain warmth of the imagination for recollection. Such persons are eager in the pursuit of some outward good to which they are attached; they are distracted by this anxious desire. They are perpetually occupied in discussions and reasoning but know nothing of that inward peace and silence that listens to God. They are more dangerous than others, because their distraction is more disguised. Search their depths, and you will find them restless, fault-finding, eager, constantly occupied with outside concerns, harsh and crude in all their desires, sensitive, full of their own thoughts, and impatient of the slightest contradiction. In a word, they are spiritual busybodies who are annoyed at everything and almost always annoying.

Letter 32: Poverty and Spoliation, the Ways of Christ

Everything contributes to prove you, but God who loves you will not suffer your temptations to exceed your strength. He will make use of the trial for your advancement.

But we must not look inward with curiosity to behold our progress, our strength, or the hand of God, which is not the less efficient because it is invisible. Its principal operations are conducted in secrecy, for we should never die to self if He always visibly stretched out His hand to save us. God would then sanctify us in light, life, and the possession of every spiritual grace, but not upon the cross in darkness, privation, nakedness, and death. The directions of Christ are not, "If any one will come after Me, let him enjoy himself; let him be gorgeously appareled; let him be intoxicated with delight, as was Peter on the mount; let him be glad in his perfection in Me and in himself; let him behold himself; and let him be assured that he is perfect." On the contrary, His words are, "*If any man will come after me* [I will show him the road he must take], *let him deny himself, and take up his cross, and follow me* [on a path beside precipices, where he will see nothing but death on every hand]" (Matthew 16:24). Saint Paul declares that we desire to be clothed, but that it is necessary, on the contrary, to be stripped to very nakedness so that we may then put on Christ.

Suffer Him, then, to despoil self-love of every adornment, even to the inmost covering under which it lurks, that you may receive the robe whitened by the blood of the Lamb and have no other purity than His. O happy soul that no longer possesses anything of its own or even anything borrowed and that abandons itself to the well beloved, being jealous of every beauty but His. O spouse, how beautiful are you when you have no longer anything of your own! You will be altogether the delight of the Bridegroom when He will be all your comeliness! Then He will love you without measure, because it will be Himself whom He loves in you.

Hear these things and believe them. This pure truth will be bitter in your mouth and belly, but it will feed your heart upon that death that is the only true life. Give faith to this and listen not to self. It is the grand seducer, more powerful than the serpent that deceived our mother. Happy is the soul that listens in all simplicity to the voice that forbids its hearing or compassionating self!

Letter 33: The Will of God Our Only Treasure

I desire that you may have that absolute simplicity of abandonment that never measures its own extent or excludes anything in the present life, no matter how dear to our self-love. All illusions come, not from such abandonment as this but from one attended by secret reservations.

Be as lowly and simple in the midst of the most exacting society as in your own closet. Do nothing from the reasoning of wisdom or from natural pleasure, but all from submission to the Spirit of life and death—life in God and death to self. Let there be no enthusiasm, no search after certainty within, no looking forward for better things, as if the present, bitter as it is, is not sufficient to those whose sole treasure is the will of God, and as if you would indemnify self-love for the sadness of the present by the prospects of the future! We deserve to meet with disappointment when we seek such vain consolation. Let us receive everything in lowliness of spirit, seeking nothing from curiosity and withholding nothing from a disguised selfishness. Let God work, and think only of dying to the present moment without reservation, as though it were the whole of eternity.

Letter 34:
Abandonment as a Simple Sinking into the Will of God

Your sole task, my dear daughter, is to bear your infirmities both of body and mind. "*When I am weak,*" says the apostle, "*then am I strong*" (2 Corinthians 12:10). Strength is made perfect in weakness. We are strong in God only to the degree that we are weak in ourselves; your feebleness will be your strength if you accept it in all lowliness.

We are tempted to believe that weakness and lowliness are incompatible with abandonment, because the latter is represented as a generous act of the soul by which it testifies its great love and makes the most heroic sacrifices. But a true abandonment does not at all correspond to this flattering description; it is a simple resting in the love of God, as an infant lies in its mother's arms. A perfect abandonment must even go as far as to abandon its abandonment. We renounce ourselves without knowing it; if we knew it, it would no longer be complete, for there can be no greater support than a consciousness that we are wholly given up.

Abandonment consists not in doing great things for self to take delight in but simply in suffering our weakness and infirmity, in letting everything alone. It is peaceful, for it would no longer be sincere if we were still restless about anything we had renounced. It is thus that abandonment is the source of true peace. If we have not peace, it is because our abandonment is exceedingly imperfect.

Letter 35:
Daily Dying Takes the Place of Final Death

We must bear our crosses. Self is the greatest of them; we are not entirely rid of it until we can tolerate ourselves as simply and as patiently as we do our neighbors. If we die in part every day of our lives, we will have but little to do on the last. What we so much dread in the future will cause us no fear when it comes if we do not suffer its terrors to be exaggerated by the restless anxieties of self-love. Bear with yourself and consent in all lowliness to be supported by your neighbor. O how utterly will these little daily deaths destroy the power of the final dying!

Letter 36:
Suffering Belongs to the Living, Not the Dead

Many are deceived when they suppose that the death of self is the cause of all the agony they feel, but their suffering is only caused by the remains of life. Pain is seated in the living, not the dead parts; the more suddenly and completely we expire, the less pain we experience. Death is painful only to him who resists it. The imagination exaggerates its terrors; the spirit argues endlessly to show the propriety of the life of self; self-love fights against death, like a sick man in the last struggle. But we must die inwardly as well as outwardly; the sentence of death has gone forth against the spirit as well as against the body. Our great care should be that the spirit dies first, and then our bodily death will be but a falling asleep. Happy are those who sleep this sleep of peace!

Letter 37: The Limits of Our Grace Are Those of Our Temptations

I sympathize sincerely with the sufferings of your dear sick one and with the pain of those whom God has placed about her to help her bear the cross. Let her not distrust God, and He will proportion her suffering to the patience that He will bestow. No one can do this but the One who made all hearts and whose office it is to renew them by His grace. The man in whom He operates knows nothing of the proper proportions, and because he is unable to see the extent of his future trials, or of the grace prepared to meet them, he is tempted to discouragement and despair. Like a man who has never seen the ocean, he stands at the coming in of the tide, between the water and an impassable wall of rock, and thinks he perceives the terrible certainty that the approaching waves must surely engulf him. He does not see that he stands within the point at which God, with unerring finger, has drawn the boundary line and beyond which the waves will not pass.

God proves the righteous as with the ocean; He stirs it up and makes its great billows seem to threaten our destruction, but He is always at hand to say, "Thus far will you go and no farther." (See Job 38:11.) *"God is faithful, who will not suffer you to be tempted above that ye are able"* (1 Corinthians 10:13).

Letter 38: Resisting God an Effectual Bar to Grace

You perceive in the depth of your conscience, by the light of God, what grace demands of you, but you resist Him. Hence your distress. You begin to say within, "It is impossible for me to undertake to do what is required of me." This is a temptation to despair. Despair as much as you please of self, but never of God; He is all good and all powerful and will grant you according to your faith. If you will believe all things, all things will be yours, and you will remove mountains. If you believe nothing, you will have nothing, but you alone will be to blame. Look at Mary, who, when the most incredible thing in the world was proposed to her, did not hesitate, but exclaimed, *"Be it unto me according to thy word"* (Luke 1:38).

Open, then, your heart. It is now so shut up that you not only have not the power to do what is required of you, but you do not even desire to have it; you have no wish that your heart should be enlarged, and you fear that it will be. How can grace find room in so straitened a heart? All that I ask of you is that you will rest in a teachable spirit of faith and that you will not listen to self. Simply acquiesce in everything with lowliness of mind, and receive peace through recollection, and everything will be gradually accomplished for you. Those things that, in your hour of temptation, seemed the greatest difficulties will be insensibly smoothed away.

Letter 39: God Speaks More Effectually in the Soul than to It

Nothing gives me more satisfaction than to see you simple and peaceful. Simplicity brings back the state of Paradise. We have no great pleasures and suffer some pain, but we have no desire for the former, and we receive the latter with thanksgiving. This interior harmony and this exemption from the fears and tormenting desires of self-love create a satisfaction in the will that is above all the joys of intoxicating delights. Dwell, then, in your terrestrial paradise and take good care not to leave it from a vain desire of knowing good and evil.

We are never less alone than when we are in the society of a single faithful friend; we are never less deserted than when we are carried in the arms of the all-powerful One. Nothing is more affecting than the instant relief of God. What He sends by means of His creatures contracts no virtue from that foul and barren channel; it owes everything to the source. And so, when the fountain breaks forth within the heart itself, we have no need of the creature. "*God, who at sundry times and in divers manners spake in time past unto the fathers by the prophets, hath in these last days spoken unto us by his Son*" (Hebrews 1:1–2). Should we then feel any regret that the feeble voice of the prophets has ceased? O how pure and powerful is the immediate voice of God in the soul! It is certain whenever Providence cuts off all the channels.

Letter 40: The Circumcision of the Heart

Our eagerness to serve others frequently arises from mere natural generosity and a refined self-love; it may soon turn into dislike and despair. But true charity is simple and ever the same toward the neighbor because it is humble and never thinks of self. Whatever is not included in this *pure charity* must be cut off.

It is by the circumcision of the heart that we are made children and inheritors of the faith of Abraham in order that we may, like him, quit our native country without knowing where we go. Blessed lot, to leave all and deliver ourselves up to the jealousy of

God, the knife of circumcision! Our own hand can cause nothing but superficial reforms; we do not know ourselves and cannot tell where to strike. We should never light upon the spot that the hand of God so readily finds. Self-love arrests our hand and spares itself; it has not the courage to wound itself to the quick. And besides, the choice of the spot and the preparation for the blow deaden its force. But the hand of God strikes in unexpected places; it finds the very joint of the harness and leaves nothing unscathed. Self-love then becomes the patient. Let it cry out, but see to it that it does not stir under the hand of God, lest it interfere with the success of the operation. It must remain motionless beneath the knife; all that is required is fidelity in not refusing a single stroke.

I am greatly attached to John the Baptist, who wholly forgot himself that he might think only of Christ; he pointed to Him. He was but the voice of one crying in the wilderness to prepare the way. He sent Him all his disciples, and it was this conduct, far more than his solitary and austere life, that entitled him to be called the greatest among those who are born of women.

Method of Prayer

By Madame Guyon

A short and very easy method of prayer that all can practice with the greatest facility and arrive in a short time by its means at a high degree of perfection.

"Walk before me, and be thou perfect."

—Genesis 17:1

CONTENTS

PREFACE

This little treatise, conceived in great simplicity, was not originally intended for publication. It was written for a few individuals who were desirous of loving God with all their hearts. Many, however, because of the profit they received in reading the manuscript, wished to obtain copies, and on this account alone, it was committed to the press.

It still remains in its original simplicity. It contains no censure on the various divine leadings of others; on the contrary, it enforces the received teachings. The whole is submitted to the judgment of the learned and experienced—requesting them, however, not to stop at the surface but to enter into the main design of the author, which is to induce the whole world to love God and to serve Him with comfort and success in a simple and easy manner, adapted to those *little* ones who are unqualified for learned and deep researches, but who earnestly desire to be truly devoted to God.

An unprejudiced reader will find hidden under the most common expressions a secret unction that will excite him to seek after that happiness that all should wish to enjoy.

In asserting that perfection is easily attained, the word *facility* is used, because God is, indeed, found with facility when we seek Him within ourselves. But some, perhaps, may reference that passage in Saint John: "*Ye shall seek me, and shall not find me*" (John 7:34). This apparent difficulty, however, is removed by another passage, where He who cannot contradict Himself has said to all, "*Seek, and ye shall find*" (Matthew 7:7). It is true, indeed, that he who would seek God, seeks Him where He is not, and therefore, it is added, *"Ye shall die in your sins"* (John 8:24). But the one who will take some trouble to seek God in his own heart and sincerely forsake his sin, that he may draw near unto Him, will infallibly find Him.

A life of piety appears so frightful to many, and prayer of such difficult attainment, that they are discouraged from taking a single step toward it. But as the apprehended difficulty of an undertaking often causes despair of succeeding and reluctance in commencing, so its desirableness and the idea that it is easy to accomplish induce us to enter upon its pursuit with pleasure, and to pursue it with vigor. The advantages and facility of this way are, therefore, set forth in the following treatise.

O were we once persuaded of the goodness of God toward His poor creatures and of His desire to communicate Himself to them, we should not create ideal monsters or so easily despair of obtaining that good that He is so earnest to bestow. *"He that spared not his own Son, but delivered him up for us all, how shall he not with him also freely give us all things?"* (Romans 8:32). It needs only a little courage and perseverance; we have enough of both in our temporal concerns, but none at all in the one thing needful. (See Luke 10:42.)

If any think God is not easily found in this way, let them not alter their minds on my testimony, but let them try it, and their own experience will convince them that the reality far exceeds all my representations of it.

Beloved reader, pursue this little tract with a sincere and candid spirit, in lowliness of mind and not with an inclination to criticize, and you will not fail to reap profit from it. It was written with a desire that you might wholly devote yourself to God. Receive it, then, with a like desire, for it has no other design than to invite the simple and the childlike to approach their father, who delights in the humble confidence of His children and is greatly grieved at their distrust. With a sincere desire, therefore, for your salvation, seek nothing but the love of God from the unpretending method here proposed, and you will assuredly obtain it.

Without setting up our opinions above those of others, we mean only with sincerity to declare, from our own experience and the experience of others, the happy effects produced by thus simply following after the Lord.

As this treatise was intended only to instruct in prayer, nothing is said of many things that we esteem, because they do not immediately relate to our main subject. It is, however, beyond a doubt that nothing will be found herein to offend, provided it be read in the spirit with which it was written. And it is still more certain that those who in right earnest make trial of the way will find we have written the truth.

It is You alone, O holy Jesus, who loves simplicity and innocence, and whose delight is to dwell with the children of men (see Proverbs 8:31), with those who are, indeed, willing to *"become as little children"* (Matthew 18:3). It is You alone who can render this little work of any value by imprinting it on the heart and leading those who read it to seek You within themselves, where You repose as in the manger, waiting to receive proofs of their love and to give them testimony of Yours. They lose these advantages by their own fault. But it belongs to You, O Child Almighty—uncreated Love, silent and all-containing Word—to make Yourself loved, enjoyed, and understood. You can do it, and I know You will do it by this little work, which belongs entirely to You, proceeds wholly from You, and tends only to You!

—*Madame Jeanne Guyon*

1

All Are Called to Prayer

On the fact that all people are called to prayer and, by the aid of ordinary grace, may put up the prayer of the heart, which is the great means of salvation, and which can be offered at all times and by the most uninstructed.

All are capable of prayer, and it is a dreadful misfortune that almost all the world has conceived the idea that they are not called to prayer. We are all called to prayer, as we are all called to salvation.

Prayer is nothing but the application of the heart to God and the internal exercise of love. Saint Paul has enjoined us to "*pray without ceasing*" (1 Thessalonians 5:17), and our Lord bids us "*watch and pray*" (Mark 13:33). All therefore may, and all ought to, practice prayer. I grant that meditation is attainable but by a few, for few are capable of it; and, therefore, my beloved brethren who are thirsty for salvation, meditative prayer is not the prayer that God requires of you or that we would recommend.

Let all pray; you should live by prayer, as you should live by love. "*I counsel thee to buy of me gold tried in the fire, that thou mayest be rich*" (Revelation 3:18). This is very easily obtained, much more easily than you can conceive.

Come, all you who are thirsty, to the living waters (see John 7:37), and do not lose your precious moments in hewing out cisterns that will hold no water (see Jeremiah 2:13). Come, you famishing souls, who find nothing to satisfy you; come, and you will be filled! Come, you poor afflicted ones, bending beneath your load of wretchedness and pain, and you will be consoled! Come, you sick, to your physician, and be not fearful of approaching Him because you are filled with diseases. Show them, and they will be healed!

Children, draw near to your Father, and He will embrace you in the arms of love! Come, you poor, stray, wandering sheep, and return to your Shepherd! Come, sinners, to your Savior! Come, you dull, ignorant, and illiterate—you who think yourselves the most incapable of prayer! You are more peculiarly called and adapted to that. Let all without exception come, for Jesus Christ has called *all.*

Yet let not those come who are without a heart; they are excused, for there must be a heart before there can be love. But who is without a heart? O come, then, give this heart to God, and here learn how to make the donation.

All who are desirous of prayer may easily pray, enabled by those ordinary graces and gifts of the Holy Spirit that are common to all men.

Prayer is the key to perfection and the sovereign good; it is the means of delivering us from every vice and obtaining for us every virtue, for the one great means of becoming perfect is to walk in the *presence* of God. He Himself has said, *"Walk before me, and be thou perfect"* (Genesis 17:1). It is by prayer alone that we are brought into His presence and maintained in it without interruption.

You must, then, learn a kind of prayer that may be exercised at all times, that does not obstruct outward employments, and that may be equally practiced by princes, kings, prelates, priests, magistrates, soldiers, children, tradesmen, laborers, women, and sick persons. It is not the prayer of the head but of the heart. It is not a prayer of the understanding alone, for the mind of man is so limited in its operations that it can have but one object at a time; but it is the prayer of the heart that is not interrupted by the exercises of reason. Nothing can interrupt this prayer but disordered affections, and when once we have enjoyed God and the sweetness of His love, we will find it impossible to relish anything but Him.

Nothing is so easily obtained as the possession and enjoyment of God. He is more present to us than we are to ourselves. He is more desirous of giving Himself to us than we are to possess Him. We need only to know how to seek Him, and the way is easier and more natural to us than breathing.

Ah, you who think yourselves so dull and fit for nothing, by prayer you may live on God Himself with less difficulty or interruption that you live on the vital air. Will it not then be highly sinful to neglect prayer? But doubtless you will not, when you have learned the method, which is the easiest in the world.

2

Prayer by Reading and Meditating

On the first degree of prayer, which is practiced in two ways—one by reading and meditation, and the other by meditation alone—as well as the rules and methods of meditation and remedies for its difficulties.

There are two ways of introducing some important practical or speculative truth, always preferring the practical and proceeding thus: Whatever truth you have chosen, read only a small portion of it, endeavoring to taste and digest it in order to extract the essence and substance of it. Proceed no further while any savor or relish remains in the passage. Then take up your book again and proceed as before, seldom reading more than half a page at a time.

It is not the quantity that is read but the manner of reading that yields us profit. Those who read fast reap no more advantage than a bee would by only skimming over the surface of the flower instead of waiting to penetrate into it and extract its sweets. Much reading is rather for scholastic subjects than divine truths; to receive profit from spiritual books, we must read as I have described, and I am certain that if that method were pursued, we should become gradually habituated to pray by our reading and more fully disposed for its exercise.

Meditation, which is the other method, is to be practiced at an appropriated season and not in the time of reading. I believe that the best manner of meditating is as follows:

When by an act of lively faith you are placed in the presence of God, read some truth wherein there is substance. Pause gently on it, not to employ the reason but merely to fix the mind, observing that the principal exercise should ever be the presence of God, and that the subject, therefore, should rather serve to stay the mind than exercise it in reasoning.

Then let a lively faith in God, immediately present in our inmost souls, produce an eager sinking into ourselves, restraining all our senses from wandering abroad. This serves to extricate us, in the first instance, from numerous constraints; to remove us far from external objects; and to bring us near to God, who is only to be found in our inmost center, which is the Holy of Holies wherein He dwells. He has even promised to come and make His abode with him who does His will. (See John 14:23.) Saint Augustine blames himself from the first for the time he lost in not having sought God in this manner of prayer.

When we are thus fully entered into ourselves and warmly penetrated throughout with a lively sense of the divine presence; when the senses are all recollected and withdrawn from the circumference to the center, and the soul is sweetly and silently employed on the truths we have read, not in reasoning but in feeding thereon and animating the will by affection rather than fatiguing the understanding by study; when, I say, the affections are in this state (which however difficult it may appear at first, is, as I will hereafter show, easily attainable)—we must allow them sweetly to repose and, as it were, swallow what they have tasted.

A person may enjoy the flavor of the finest foods in chewing, yet receive no nourishment from them if he does not cease the action and swallow the food. So, when our affections are enkindled, if we endeavor to stir them up yet more, we extinguish the flame, and the soul is deprived of its nourishment. We should, therefore, in a repose of love, full of respect and confidence, swallow the blessed food we have received. This method is highly necessary and will advance the soul more in a short time than any other method will do in years.

But as I have said that our direct and principal exercise should consist in the contemplation of the divine presence, we should be exceedingly diligent in recalling our dissipated senses as the most easy method of overcoming distractions; for a direct contest only serves to irritate and augment them; while, by sinking within under a view by faith of a present God and simply recollecting ourselves, we wage insensibly a very successful, though indirect, war with them.

It is proper here to caution beginners against wandering from truth to truth and from subject to subject. The right way to penetrate every divine truth, to enjoy its full relish, and to imprint it on the heart is to dwell upon it while its savor continues.

Though recollection is difficult in the beginning, because of the habit the soul has acquired of being always abroad, yet, when by the violence it has done itself, it becomes a little accustomed to it, the process is soon rendered perfectly easy. This is partly from the force of habit, and partly because God, whose one will toward His creatures is to communicate Himself to them, imparts abundant grace and an experimental enjoyment of His presence, which very much facilitate it.

3

A Method of Meditative Prayer

On a method of meditative prayer for those who cannot read—applied to the Lord's Prayer and to some of the attributes of God—and on transition from the first to the second degree of prayer.

Those who cannot read books are not, on that account, excluded from prayer. The great book that teaches all things and that is written all over, within and without, is Jesus Christ Himself.

The method they should practice is this: They should first learn this fundamental truth, that "*the kingdom of God is within you*" (Luke 17:21) and that it must be sought there only.

It is as incumbent on the clergy to instruct their parishioners in prayer as in their catechism. It is true they tell them the end of their creation, but they do not give them sufficient instructions on how they may attain it.

They should be taught to begin by an act of profound adoration and annihilation before God and, closing the corporeal eyes, endeavor to open those of the soul. They should then collect themselves inwardly and, by a lively faith in God, as dwelling within them, pierce into the divine presence, not allowing the senses to wander abroad, but holding them as much as may be in subjection.

They should then repeat the Lord's Prayer in their native tongue, pondering a little upon the meaning of the words and the infinite willingness of the God who dwells within them to become, indeed, their Father. In this state, let them pour out their wants before Him, and when they have pronounced the word *Father*, let them remain a few moments in a reverential silence, waiting to have the will of this their heavenly Father made manifest to them.

Again, the Christian, beholding himself in the state of a feeble child, soiled and sorely bruised by repeated falls, destitute of strength to stand or of power to cleanse himself, should lay his deplorable situation open to his Father's view in humble confusion, occasionally intermingling a word or two of love and grief, and then again sinking into silence before Him. Then, continuing the Lord's Prayer, let him beseech this King of Glory to reign in him, abandoning himself to God and acknowledging His right to rule over him, so that He may do it.

If he feels an inclination to peace and silence, let him not continue the words of the prayer so long as this sensation holds, and when it subsides, let him go on with the second petition, "*Thy will be done in earth, as it is in heaven*" (Matthew 6:10). With this, let these humble supplicants beseech God to accomplish in them and by them all His will, and let them surrender their hearts and freedom into His hands to be disposed of as He pleases. When they find that the will should be employed in loving, they will desire to love and will implore Him for His love. But all this will take place sweetly and peacefully, and so of the rest of the prayer, in which the clergy may instruct them.

But they should not burden themselves with frequent repetitions of set forms or studied prayers, for the Lord's Prayer once repeated, as I have just described, will produce abundant fruit.

At other times, they may place themselves as sheep before their Shepherd, looking up to Him for their true food. They may say something like, "O divine Shepherd, You feed Your flock with Yourself, and are, indeed, their daily bread." They may also represent to Him the needs of their families, but let all be done from this principal and one great view of faith, that God is within them.

All our imaginations of God amount to nothing; a lively faith in His presence is sufficient. For we must not form any image of the Deity, though we may of Jesus Christ, beholding Him in His birth or His crucifixion or in some other state or mystery, provided the soul always seeks Him in its own center.

On other occasions, we may look to Him as a physician and present for His healing virtue all our maladies, but always without perturbation and with pauses from time to time, that the silence, being mingled with action, may be gradually extended and our own exertion lessened until at length, as we continually yield to God's operations, He gains the complete ascendancy, as will be hereafter explained.

When the divine presence is granted us and we gradually begin to relish silence and repose, this experimental enjoyment of the presence of God introduces the soul into the second degree of prayer, which, by proceeding in the manner I have described, is attainable by the illiterate as well as by the learned; some privileged souls, indeed, are favored with it even from the beginning.

4

The Prayer of Simplicity

On the second degree of prayer, called here the "prayer of simplicity," and on what time we reach it, how to offer and continue it, and the requisites for offering it acceptably.

Some call the second degree of prayer "contemplation," or the "prayer of faith and stillness," while others call it the "prayer of simplicity." I will here use this latter appellation, as being more accurate than that of contemplation, which implies a more advanced state of prayer than that I am now treating of.

When the soul has been for some time exercised in the way I have mentioned, it gradually finds that it is enabled to approach God with facility, that recollection is attended with much less difficulty, and that prayer becomes easy, sweet, and delightful. It recognizes that this is the true way of finding God and feels that "[His] *name is as ointment poured forth*" (Song of Solomon 1:3). The method must now be altered, and that which I describe must be pursued with courage and fidelity, without being disturbed at the difficulties we may encounter in the way.

First, as soon as the soul by faith places itself in the presence of God and becomes recollected before Him, let it remain thus for a little time in respectful silence.

But if, at the beginning, in forming the act of faith, it feels some little pleasing sense of the divine presence, let it remain there without being troubled for a subject and proceed no further, but carefully cherish this sensation while it continues. When it abates, it may excite the will by some tender affection, and if, by the first moving thereof, it finds itself reinstated in sweet peace, let it there remain. The fire must be gently fanned, but as soon as it is kindled, we must cease our efforts, lest we extinguish it by our activity.

I would warmly recommend to all never to finish prayer without remaining some little time afterward in a respectful silence. It is also of the greatest importance for the soul to approach prayer with courage and to bring with it such a pure and disinterested love as seeks nothing from God but to please Him and to do His will; for a servant who only proportions his diligence to his hope of reward is unworthy of any recompense. Go then to prayer, not desiring to enjoy spiritual delights, but to be just as it pleases God; this will preserve your spirit tranquil in dryness, as well as in consolation, and prevent you from being surprised at the apparent repulses or absence of God.

5

Deprivation of the Sensible Presence of God

On various matters occurring in or belonging to the degree of prayer (that is to say, on dryness, which is caused by deprivation of the sensible presence of God for an admirable end, and which is to be met by acts of solid and peaceful virtue of the mind and soul), and on the advantages of this course.

Though God has no other desire than to impart Himself to the loving soul that seeks Him, He frequently conceals Himself from it, that it may be roused from sloth and impelled to seek Him with fidelity and love. But with what abundant goodness does He recompense the faithfulness of His beloved! And how often are these apparent withdrawings of Himself succeeded by the caresses of love!

At these seasons, we are apt to believe that it proves our fidelity and evinces a greater ardor of affection to seek Him by an exertion of our own strength and activity, or that such a course will induce Him the more speedily to revisit us. No, dear souls, believe me; this is not the best way in this degree of prayer. With patient love, with self-abasement and humiliation, with the reiterated breathings of an ardent but peaceful affection, and with silence full of veneration, you must await the return of the Beloved.

Thus only can you demonstrate that it is Him alone and His good pleasure that you seek and not the selfish delights of your own sensations in loving Him. Hence it is said, "Be not impatient in the time of dryness and obscurity; suffer the suspensions and delays of the consolations of God; cleave unto Him, and wait upon Him patiently, so that your life may increase and be renewed." (See Sirach 2:2–3 RSV.)

Be patient in prayer, though during your whole lifetime you should do nothing else than wait for the return of the Beloved in a spirit of humiliation, abandonment, contentment, and resignation. This is a most excellent prayer, and it may be intermingled with the sighs of plaintive love! This conduct indeed is most pleasing to the heart of God, and will, above all others, compel His return.

6

The Abandonment of Self to God

On the abandonment of self to God, its fruit and its irrevocableness, its nature, the fact that God requires it, and its practice.

Here we must begin to abandon ourselves and to give up our whole existence to God, from the strong and positive conviction that the occurrences of every moment result from His immediate will and permission, and are just such as our state requires. This conviction will make us content with everything and cause us to regard all that happens, not from the side of the creature, but from that of God.

But, dearly beloved, whoever you are who sincerely wishes to give yourselves up to God, I conjure you, that after having once made the donation, you do not take yourselves back again. Remember, a gift once presented is no longer at the disposal of the giver.

Abandonment is a matter of the greatest importance in our progress; it is the key to the inner court, so that he who knows truly how to abandon himself will soon become perfect. We must, therefore, continue steadfast and immovable therein, without listening to the voice of natural reason. Great faith produces great abandonment; we must confide in God, hoping against hope. (See Romans 4:18.)

Abandonment is the casting off of all selfish care so that we may be altogether at divine disposal. All Christians are exhorted to abandon themselves, for it is said to all:

> *Your heavenly Father knoweth that ye have need of all these things. . . . Take therefore no thought for the morrow.* (Matthew 6:32, 34)

> *In all thy ways acknowledge him, and he shall direct thy paths.* (Proverbs 3:6)

> *Commit thy works unto the* Lord*, and thy thoughts shall be established.* (Proverbs 16:3)

> *Commit thy way unto the* Lord*; trust also in him; and he shall bring it to pass.* (Psalm 37:5)

Our abandonment, then, should be, both in respect to external and internal things, an absolute giving up of all our concerns into the hands of God, forgetting ourselves and thinking only of Him, by which the heart will remain always disengaged, free, and at peace.

It is practiced by continually losing our own will in the will of God and renouncing every private inclination as soon as it arises, however good it may appear, so that we may stand in indifference with respect to ourselves, and only will what God has willed from all eternity. We must be resigning ourselves in all things, whether for soul or body, for time or eternity; forgetting the past, leaving the future to Providence, and devoting the present to God. We must be satisfied with the present moment, which brings with it God's eternal order in reference to us, and is as infallible a declaration of His will as it is inevitable and common to all; and we must attribute nothing that befalls us to the creature, but regard all things in God, looking upon all (except only our sins) as infallibly proceeding from Him.

Surrender yourselves then to be led and disposed of just as God pleases, with respect both to your outward and inward state.

7

The Use, Profit, and Practice of Suffering

On the use, profit, and practice of suffering, and that it should be accepted from the hand of God.

Be patient under all the sufferings God sends. If your love for Him be pure, you will not seek Him less on Calvary than on Tabor. And surely, He should be as much loved on that as on this, since it was on Calvary that He made the greatest display of love.

Be not as those who give themselves to Him at one season, only to withdraw from Him at another. They give themselves only to be caressed, and they pull themselves back again when they are crucified (or at least turn for consolation to the creature).

No, beloved souls, you will not find consolation in anything but in the love of the cross and in total abandonment. The one who does not savor the cross does not savor the things that are of God. (See Matthew 16:23.) It is impossible to love God without loving the cross, and a heart that savors the cross finds the bitterest things to be sweet (see Proverbs 27:7), because it finds itself hungering for God in proportion to its hungering for the cross. God gives us the cross, and the cross gives us God. We may be assured that there is an internal advancement when there is progress in the way of the cross; abandonment and the cross go hand in hand.

As soon as anything is presented in the form of suffering and you feel repugnance, resign yourself immediately to God with respect to it, and give yourself up to Him in sacrifice. You will then find that when the cross arrives, it will not be as very burdensome because you have yourself desired it. This, however, does not prevent you from feeling its weight, as some have imagined, for when we do not feel the cross, we do not suffer. A sensibility to suffering is one of the principal parts of suffering itself. Jesus Christ Himself chose to endure its utmost rigors. We often bear the cross in weakness, at other times in strength. All should be alike to us in the will of God.

8

The Mysteries of God

On mysteries, and the fact that God gives them in this state in reality, and that we must let Him bestow or withhold them as seems good to Him, with a loving regard to His will.

It will be objected that, by this method, we will have no mysteries imprinted on our minds, but this is so far from being the case; it is, in fact, the peculiar means of imparting them to the soul. Jesus Christ, to whom we are abandoned, whom we follow as the way, whom we hear as the truth, and who animates us as the life by imprinting Himself on the soul, impresses there the characters of His different states. To bear all the states of Jesus Christ is a much greater thing than to merely meditate about them. Saint Paul said, "*I bear in my body the marks of the Lord Jesus*" (Galatians 6:17); he does not say that he reasoned thereon.

In this state of abandonment, Jesus Christ frequently communicates some peculiar views or revelations of His states. These we should thankfully accept, and dispose ourselves for what appears to be His will, receiving equally whatever frame He may bestow, and having no other choice but that of ardently reaching after Him, of dwelling ever with Him, of sinking into nothingness before Him, and of accepting indiscriminately all His gifts, whether darkness or illumination, fecundity or barrenness, weakness or strength, sweetness or bitterness, temptations, distractions, pain, weariness, or uncertainty. And none of all these should, for one moment, slow our course.

God engages some, for whole years, in the contemplation and enjoyment of a single mystery, the simple view or contemplation of which recollects the soul. Let them be faithful to it. But as soon as God is pleased to withdraw this view from the soul, let it freely yield to the deprivation. Some are very uneasy at their inability to meditate on certain mysteries, but without reason, since an affectionate attachment to God includes in itself every kind of devotion, and whoever is calmly united to God alone is, indeed, most excellently and effectually applied to every divine mystery. Whoever loves God loves all that appertains to Him.

9

Virtues from God in the Heart

On virtue and the fact that all virtues come with God and are solidly and deeply implanted in the soul in this degree by the prayer of the heart, which takes place without difficulty.

It is thus that we acquire virtue with facility and certainty, for as God is the principle of all virtues, we inherit all in the possession of Him. And to the extent that we approach toward His possession, we receive the most eminent virtues; for all virtue is but as a mask, an outside appearance that is as mutable as our garments if it is not bestowed from within. Then, indeed, it is genuine, essential, and permanent. David says, "*The king's daughter is all glorious within*" (Psalm 45:13). These souls, above all others, practice virtue in the most eminent degree, though they advert not to any particular virtue. God, to whom they are united, leads them to the most extensive practice of it. He is exceedingly jealous over them and permits them not the least pleasure.

What a hungering for sufferings have those souls, who thus glow with divine love! How would they precipitate themselves into excessive austerities, where they are permitted to pursue their own inclinations! They think of nothing except how they may please their Beloved, and they begin to neglect and forget themselves, and as their love for God increases, so do self-detestation and disregard of the creature.

O were this simple method once acquired, a way so suited to all, to the dull and ignorant as well as to the most learned, how easily would the whole church of God be reformed! Love only is required. "Love," says Saint Augustine, "and then do what you please." For when we truly love, we cannot have so much as a will to do anything that might offend the object of our affections.

10

Perfecting Mortification by Dwelling on God

On mortification and the fact that it is never perfect when it is solely exterior but must be accomplished by dwelling upon God within, and that this, however, does not dispense with its outward practice to some degree, hence leading to a sound conversion.

I say further, that, in any other way, it is next to impossible to acquire a perfect mortification of the senses and passions.

The reason is obvious: The soul gives vigor and energy to the senses, and the senses raise and stimulate the passions. A dead body has neither sensations nor passions, because its connection with the soul is dissolved. All endeavors merely to rectify the exterior impel the soul yet farther outward into that about which it is so warmly and zealously engaged. Its powers are diffused and scattered abroad; for, its whole attention being immediately directed to austerities and other externals, it thus invigorates those very senses it is aiming to subdue. For the senses have no other spring from which to derive their vigor than the application of the soul to themselves, the degree of their life and activity being proportioned to the degree of attention that the soul bestows upon them. This life of the senses stirs up and provokes the passions, instead of suppressing or subduing them; austerities may indeed enfeeble the body, but for the reasons just mentioned, can never lessen the keenness of the senses nor their activity.

The only method of causing this is inward recollection, by which the soul is turned wholly and altogether inward to possess a present God. If it directs all its vigor and energy within, this simple act separates it from the senses, and employing all its powers internally, it renders them faint. The nearer it draws to God, the farther is it separated from self. Hence it is that those in whom the attractions of grace are very powerful find the outward man altogether weak and feeble and even liable to fainting.

I do not mean by this to discourage mortification, for it should ever accompany prayer, according to the strength and state of the person or as obedience demands. But I say that mortification should not be our principal exercise. Neither should we prescribe to ourselves such and such austerities, but as we simply follow the internal attractions of grace and are occupied with the divine presence, without thinking particularly on mortification, God will enable us to perform every kind of it. He gives those who abide faithful to their abandonment to Him no relaxation until He has subdued everything in them that remains to be mortified.

We have only, then, to continue steadfast in the utmost attention to God, and all things will be perfectly done. All are not capable of outward austerities, but all are capable of this. In the mortification of the eye and ear, which continually supply the busy imagination with new subjects, there is little danger of falling into excess, but God will teach us this also. We need only to follow His Spirit.

The soul has a double advantage by proceeding thus, for in withdrawing from outward objects, it constantly draws nearer to God, and besides the secret sustaining and preserving power and virtue that it receives, it is farther removed from sin the nearer it comes to Him, so that its conversion becomes firmly established as a matter of habit.

11

Perfect Conversion

On the perfect conversion that is the result of this kind of prayer and how it is accomplished, as well as two of its aids—the drawing of God and the tendency of the soul to its center—and its practice.

"Turn ye unto him from whom the children of Israel have deeply revolted."
—Isaiah 31:6

Conversion is nothing more than turning away from the creature in order to return to God.

It is not perfect (however good and essential to salvation) when it consists simply in turning from sin to grace. To be complete, it should take place from without inwardly.

When the soul is once turned toward God, it finds a wonderful facility in continuing steadfast in conversion, and the longer it remains thus converted, the nearer it approaches and the more firmly it adheres to God. And the nearer it draws to Him, it is of necessity farther removed from the creature, which is so contrary to Him, so that it is effectually established in conversion that the state becomes habitual and, as it were, natural.

Now, we must not suppose that this is effected by a violent exertion of its own powers; for it is not capable of it, nor should it attempt any other co-operation with divine grace than that of endeavoring to withdraw itself from external objects and to turn inward, after which it has nothing further to do than to continue firm in its adherence to God.

God has an attractive virtue that draws the soul more and more powerfully to Himself, and in attracting us, He purifies us, just as it is with a gross vapor exhaled by the sun, which, as it gradually ascends, is rarified and rendered pure. The vapor, indeed, contributes to its ascent only by its passivity, but the soul co-operates freely and voluntarily.

This kind of introversion is very easy and advances the soul naturally and without effort, because God is our center. The center always exerts a very powerful attractive virtue, and the more spiritual and exalted it is, the more violent and irresistible are its attractions.

But besides the attracting virtue of the center, there is, in every creature, *a strong tendency to reunite* with its center, which is vigorous and active in proportion to the spirituality and perfection of the subject.

As soon as anything is turned toward its center, it is precipitated toward it with extreme rapidity, unless it is withheld by some invincible obstacle. A stone held in the hand is no sooner disengaged than by its own weight it falls to the earth as to its center; so also water and fire, when unobstructed, flow incessantly toward their center. Now, when the soul by its efforts to recollect itself is brought into the influence of the central tendency, it falls gradually, without any other force than the weight of love, into its proper center. And the more passive and tranquil it remains, the freer from self-motion it is, and the more rapidly it advances because the energy of the central attractive virtue is unobstructed and has full liberty for action.[6]

All our care should, therefore, be directed toward acquiring the greatest degree of inward recollection. Neither should we be discouraged by the difficulties we encounter in this exercise, which will soon be recompensed on the part of God by such abundant supplies of grace as will render it perfectly easy, provided that we are faithful in meekly withdrawing our hearts from outward distractions and occupations, and returning to our center with affections full of tenderness and serenity. When at any time the passions are turbulent, a gentle retreat inward to a present God easily deadens them; any other way of opposing rather irritates than appeases them.

---

6. Note from the editor: This beautiful image comprehends the whole essence of the divine life, as understood by the teachers of the interior, and it seems to contain as much truth as beauty. God is the great magnet of the soul, but of that only, and impurity or mixture prevents His full attractive power. If there was nothing of the kind in the soul, it would rush, under this all-powerful attraction, with irresistible and instantaneous speed, to be lost in God. But many load themselves with goods or seize some part of earth or self with so tenacious a grasp that they spend their whole lives without advancing at more than a snail's pace toward their center, and it is only when God in love strikes their burden violently from their hands that they begin to be conscious of the hindrance that detained them. If we will only suffer every weight to drop and withdraw our hands from self and every creature, there will be but little interval between our sacrifice and our resurrection. Some pious persons have objected to the passivity here inculcated, as though the soul were required to become dead, like an inanimate object, in order that God might do His pleasure with it. But this objection will vanish if it be considered that the life of the soul is in the will and that this condition of utter passivity implies the highest state of activity of the will, in willing without any cessation and with all its powers that the will of God shall be done in it and by it and through it. See this further insisted upon in chapter 21.

12

The Prayer of Silence

On another and more exalted degree of prayer—the prayer of the simple presence of God or of active contemplation (of which very little is said, the subject being reserved for another treatise); on how selfish activity merges here in an activity lively, full, abundant, divine, easy, and as it were natural—a state far different from that idleness and passivity objected to by the opponents of the inner life—the subject being illustrated by several comparisons; on the transition to infused prayer, in which the fundamental, vital activity of the soul is not lost but is more abundantly and powerfully influenced (as are the faculties) by that of God; and on the facility of these methods of coming to God, and an exhortation to self-abandonment.

The soul that is faithful in the exercise of love and adherence to God is astonished to feel Him gradually taking possession of its whole being; it now enjoys a continual sense of that presence that has become, as it were, natural to it. And this, as well as prayer, becomes a matter of habit. It feels an unusual serenity gradually diffusing itself over all its faculties. Silence now constitutes its whole prayer, while God communicates an infused love, which is the beginning of ineffable blessedness.

O that I was permitted to pursue this subject and describe some degrees of the endless progression of subsequent states! But I now write only for beginners, and will, therefore, proceed no further, but wait for our Lord's time to develop what may be applicable to every state.[7]

We must, however, urge it as a matter of the highest import to cease self-action and self-exertion so that God Himself may act alone. He says by the mouth of His prophet David, "*Be still, and know that I am God*" (Psalm 46:10). But the center is so infatuated with love and attachment to its own working that it does not believe that it works at all unless it can feel, know, and distinguish all its operations. It is ignorant that its inability minutely to observe the manner of its motion is occasioned by the swiftness of its progress, and that the operations of God, abounding more and more, absorb those of the creature, just as we see that the stars shine brightly before the sun rises, but gradually vanish as his light advances, and become invisible, not from want of light in themselves, but from the excess of it in him.

The case is similar here, for there is a strong and universal light that absorbs all the little distinct lights of the soul; they grow faint and disappear under its powerful influence, and self-activity is now no longer distinguishable.

Those who accuse this prayer of inactivity greatly err, a charge that can only arise from inexperience. O if they would but make some efforts toward the attainment of it, they would soon become full of light and knowledge in relation to it.

This appearance of inaction is, indeed, not the consequence of sterility but of abundance, as will be clearly perceived by the experienced soul, who will recognize that the silence is full and unctuous by reason of plenty.

There are two kinds of people who keep silent: the one keeps silent because they have nothing to say, and the other because they

7. Note from the editor: A design subsequently carried out in the work entitled *The Torrents* and less diffusely in the *Concise View* follows the present treatise.

have too much to say. The latter is the case in this state; silence is occasioned by excess and not by defect.

To be drowned and to die of thirst are deaths widely different, yet water may be said to be the cause of both. Abundance destroys in one case, and want in the other. So here the fullness of grace stills the activity of self, and therefore, it is of the utmost importance to remain as silent as possible.

The infant at its mother's breast is a lively illustration of our subject; it begins to draw the milk by moving its little lips, but when its nourishment flows abundantly, it is content to swallow without effort. By any other course, it would only hurt itself, spill the milk, and be obliged to quit the breast.

We must act in like manner when beginning to pray by moving the lips of the affections, but as soon as the milk of divine grace flows freely, we have nothing to do but, in stillness, sweetly imbibe and, when it ceases to flow, again stir up the affections as an infant moves its lips. Whoever acts otherwise cannot make the best use of this grace, which is bestowed to allure the soul into the repose of love and not to force it into the multiplicity of self.

But what becomes of the babe who thus gently and without exertion drinks in the milk? Who would believe that it could thus receive nourishment? Yet the more peacefully it feeds, the better it thrives. What, I say, becomes of this infant? It drops asleep on its mother's bosom. So the soul that is tranquil and peaceful in prayer sinks frequently into a mystic slumber, wherein all its powers are at rest till it is wholly fitted for that state, of which it enjoys these transient anticipations. You see that in this process the soul is led naturally, without trouble, effort, art, or study.

The interior is not a stronghold, to be taken by storm and violence but a kingdom of peace that is to be gained only by love. If any will thus pursue the little path I have pointed out, it will lead them to "infused" prayer. God demands nothing extraordinary or too difficult; on the contrary, He is greatly pleased by a simple and childlike conduct.

The most sublime attainments in religion are those that are easiest reached; the most necessary ordinances are the least difficult. It is thus also in natural things. If you would reach the sea, embark on a river, and you will be conveyed to it insensibly and without exertion. If you want to go to God, follow this sweet and simple path, and you will arrive at the desired object with an ease and expedition that will amaze you.

O that you would but once make the trial! How soon you would find that all I have said is too little and that your own experience will carry you infinitely beyond it! What is it you fear? Why do you not instantly cast yourself into the arms of love or the One who extended them on the cross, that He might embrace you? What risk do you run in depending solely on God and abandoning yourself wholly to Him? Ah, He will not deceive you, unless by bestowing an abundance beyond your highest hopes. But those who expect all from themselves may hear this rebuke of God by His prophet Isaiah, "*Thou art wearied in the greatness of thy way; yet saidst thou not, There is no hope: thou hast found the life of thine hand; therefore thou wast not grieved*" (Isaiah 57:10).

13

Peaceful Rest in the Soul

On the rest before God present in the soul in a wonderful way, as well as fruits of this peaceful presence and practical advice.

The soul advanced thus far has no need of any other preparation than its quietude, for now the presence of God during the day, which is the great effect, or rather the continuation of prayer, begins to be infused, and almost without intermission. The soul certainly enjoys transcendent blessedness and finds that God is more intimately present to it than it is to itself.

The only way to find Him is by introversion. No sooner do the bodily eyes close than the soul is wrapped in prayer; it is amazed at so great a blessing and enjoys an internal converse that external matters cannot interrupt.

The same may be said of this kind of prayer that is said of wisdom: "*All good things came to me along with her*" (Wisdom 7:11 RSV). For virtues flow from this soul into exercise with so much sweetness and facility that they appear natural to it, and the living spring within breaks forth abundantly into a facility for all goodness and an insensibility to all evil.

Let it then remain faithful in this state and beware of choosing or seeking any other disposition whatever than this simple rest, as a preparative either to confession or communion, to action or prayer. For its sole business is to allow itself to be filled with this divine effusion. I would not be understood to speak of the preparations necessary for ordinances but of the most interior disposition in which they can be received.

14

An Inner Silence

On interior silence; its reason; the fact that God recommends it; and the reality that exterior silence, retirement, and recollection contribute to it.

"The Lord is in his holy temple:
let all the earth keep silence before him."

—Habakkuk 2:20

The reason why inner silence is so indispensable is because the Word is essential and eternal and necessarily requires dispositions in the soul in some degree correspondent to God's nature, as a capacity for the reception of Himself. Hearing is a sense formed to receive sounds and is rather passive than active, admitting, but not communicating, sensation. And if we would hear, we must lend our ears for that purpose. Christ, the eternal Word, who must be communicated to the soul to give it new life, requires the most intense attention to His voice when He would speak within us.

Hence it is so frequently enjoined upon us in Scripture to listen and be attentive to the voice of God. I quote a few of the numerous exhortations to this effect:

> *Hearken unto me, my people; and give ear unto me, O my nation.* (Isaiah 51:4)

> *Hearken unto me...*[all ye] *which are borne by me from the belly, which are carried from the womb.* (Isaiah 46:3)

> *Hearken, O daughter, and consider, and incline thine ear; forget also thine own people, and thy father's house; so shall the king greatly desire thy beauty.* (Psalm 45:10–11)

We must forget ourselves and all self-interest, and listen and be attentive to God; these two simple actions, or rather passive dispositions, produce the love of that beauty which He Himself communicates.

Outward silence is very requisite for the cultivation and improvement of inward silence, and indeed, it is impossible that we should become truly interior without loving silence and retirement. God says by the mouth of His prophet Hosea, "*Therefore, behold, I will allure her, and bring her into the wilderness* [in solitude], *and speak comfortably unto her*" (Hosea 2:14). And unquestionably, the being internally engaged with God is wholly incompatible with being externally busied about a thousand trifles.

When through weakness we become, as it were, uncentered, we must immediately turn again inward, and this process we must repeat as often as our distractions recur. It is a small matter to be devout and recollected for an hour or half hour if the unction and spirit of prayer do not continue with us throughout the whole day.

15

Examination of the Conscience

On the examination of conscience (how it is performed in this state and that by God Himself); on the confession, contrition, and forgetfulness or remembrance of faults in this state; and on the fact that this is not applicable to the previous degree: communion.

Self-examination should always precede confession, but the manner of it should be conformable to the state of the soul. The business of those who are advanced to the degree of which we now treat is to lay their whole souls open before God, who will not fail to enlighten them and enable them to see the peculiar nature of their faults. This examination, however, should be peaceful and tranquil, and we should depend on God for the discovery and knowledge of our sins rather than on the diligence of our own scrutiny.

When we examine with effort, we are easily deceived and betrayed by self-love into error, "*call*[ing] *evil good, and good evil*" (Isaiah 5:20); but when we lie in full exposure before the Sun of Righteousness, His divine beams render the smallest atoms visible. Then we must forsake self and abandon our souls to God in examination as well as confession.

When souls have attained to this species of prayer, no fault escapes the reprehension of God. No sooner are they committed than they are rebuked by an inward burning and tender confusion; such is the scrutiny of Him who suffers no evil to be concealed. And the only way is to turn simply to God and bear the pain and correction He inflicts.

As He becomes the incessant examiner of the soul, it can now no longer examine itself, and if it be faithful in its abandonment, experience will prove that it is much more effectually explored by His divine light than by all its own carefulness.

Those who tread these paths should be informed of a matter respecting their confusion, in which they are apt to err. When they begin to give an account of their sins, instead of the regret and contrition they had been accustomed to feel, they find that love and tranquility sweetly pervade and take possession of their souls. Now those who are not properly instructed are desirous of resisting this sensation and forming an act of contrition because they have heard, with truth, that this is requisite. But they are not aware that they thereby lose the genuine contrition, which is this infused love, and which infinitely surpasses any effect produced by self-exertion, comprehending the other acts in itself as in one principal act, in much higher perfection than if they were distinctly perceived.

Let them not be troubled to do otherwise when God acts so excellently in and for them. To hate sin in this manner is to hate it as God does. The purest love is that which is of His immediate operation in the soul. Why should we then be so eager for action? Let us remain in the state He assigns us, agreeable to the instructions of the wise man: "Put your confidence in God; remain in quiet where he hath placed you."

The soul will also be amazed at finding a difficulty in calling its faults to remembrance. This, however, should cause no uneasiness.

First, because this forgetfulness of our faults is some proof of our purification from them, and in this degree of advancement, it is best to forget whatever concerns ourselves that we may remember only God. Second, because when confession is our duty, God will not fail to make known to us our greatest faults; for then He Himself examines us, and the soul will feel the end of examination more perfectly accomplished than it could possibly have been by all our own endeavors.

These instructions, however, would be altogether unsuitable to the preceding degrees, while the soul continues in its active state, wherein it is right and necessary that it should in all things exert itself in proportion to its advancement. As to those who have arrived at this more advanced state, I exhort them to follow these instructions and to not vary their simple occupations even on approaching the communion. Let them remain in silence and suffer God to act freely. He cannot be better received than by Himself.

16

Reading and Vocal Prayers

On reading and vocal prayers; they should be limited and should not be used against our interior drawing, unless they are of obligation.

The method of reading in this state is to cease when you feel yourself recollected and remain in stillness, reading but little and always desisting when thus internally attracted.

The soul that is called to a state of inward silence should not encumber itself with vocal prayers. Whenever it makes use of them, and finds a difficulty therein, and an attraction to silence, let it not use constraint by persevering, but yield to the internal drawing, unless the repeating of such prayers be a matter of obligation. In any other case, it is much better not to set forms but to be wholly given up to the leadings of the Holy Spirit; and in this way, every kind of devotion is fulfilled in a most eminent degree.

17

Petitions of the Spirit of God

On petitions, that those of self-origin should cease and their place be taken by those of the Spirit of God, which requires abandonment and faith.

The soul should not be surprised at feeling itself unable to offer up to God such petitions as had formerly been made with facility, for now the Spirit that helps in our infirmities makes intercession for it according to the will of God, "*for we know not what we should pray for as we ought: but the Spirit itself maketh intercession for us with groanings which cannot be uttered*" (Romans 8:26). We must second the designs of God, which tend to free us of all our own operations, so that His may be substituted in their place.

Let this, then, be done in you, and suffer not yourself to be attached to anything, however good it may appear; it is no longer such to you if it, in any measure, turns you aside from what God desires of you. For the divine will is preferable to every other good. Shake off, then, all self-interest, and live by faith and abandonment. Here it is that genuine faith begins truly to operate.

18

Turning from Faults to God

On faults committed in the state, that we must turn from them to God without trouble or discouragement, and that the contrary course weakens us and is opposed to the practice of humble souls.

Should we either wander among externals or commit a fault, we must instantly turn inward, for having departed thereby from God, we should turn toward Him as soon as possible and suffer the penalty that He inflicts.

It is of great importance to guard against vexation on account of our faults; it springs from a secret root of pride and a love of our own excellence. We are hurt at feeling what we are.

If we become discouraged, we are the more enfeebled, and from our reflections on our imperfections, a chagrin arises that is often worse than the imperfections themselves.

The truly humble soul is not surprised at its defects or failings, and the more miserable it beholds itself, the more it abandons itself to God and presses for a more intimate alliance with Him, seeing the need it has of His aid. We should rather be induced to act thus, as God Himself has said, *"I will instruct thee and teach thee in the way which thou shalt go: I will guide thee with mine eye"* (Psalm 32:8).

19

The Remedy for Distractions and Temptations

On distractions and temptations, the remedy of which is to turn to God, which is the practice of the saints, since there is danger in any other way.

A direct struggle with distractions and temptations rather serves to augment them and withdraws the soul from that adherence to God that should ever be its sole occupation. We should simply turn away from the evil and draw yet nearer to God. A little child, on perceiving a monster, does not wait to fight with it, and will scarcely turn its eyes toward it, but will quickly shrink into the bosom of its mother in assurance of its safety. The psalmist says, "*God is in the midst of her; she shall not be moved: God shall help her, and that right early*" (Psalm 46:5).

If we do otherwise and in our weakness attempt to attack our enemies, we will frequently find ourselves wounded, if not totally defeated. But by remaining in the simple presence of God, we will find instant supplies of strength for our support. This was the resource of David, who says, "*I have set the Lord always before me: because he is at my right hand, I shall not be moved. Therefore my heart is glad, and my glory rejoiceth: my flesh also shall rest in hope*" (Psalm 16:8–9). And it is said in Exodus, "*The Lord shall fight for you, and ye shall hold your peace*" (Exodus 14:14).

20

Prayer as a Devotional Sacrifice

On prayer divinely explained as a devotional sacrifice under the similitude of incense, on our annihilation in this sacrifice, and on the solidity and fruit of this prayer according to the gospel.

Both devotion and sacrifice are comprehended in prayer, which, according to Saint John, is an incense, the smoke of which ascends to God. Therefore it is said in Revelation that "*there was given unto* [the angel] *much incense, that he should offer it with the prayers of all saints*" (Revelation 8:3).

Prayer is the effusion of the heart in the presence of God. Hannah the mother of Samuel said, "*I...have poured out my soul before the Lord*" (1 Samuel 1:15). The prayer of the wise men at the feet of Christ in the stable of Bethlehem was signified by the incense they offered.

Prayer has a certain warmth of love—melting, dissolving, and sublimating the soul, and causing it to ascend unto God; and as the soul is melted, odors rise from it, and these sweet exhalations proceed from the consuming fire of love within.

This is illustrated in the Song of Solomon 1:12, where the spouse says, "*While the king sitteth at his table, my spikenard sendeth forth the smell thereof.*" The table is the center of the soul, and when God is there, and we know how to dwell near Him and abide with Him, the sacred presence gradually dissolves the hardness of the soul. As it melts, fragrance issues forth. Hence it is that the Beloved says of his spouse, in seeing her soul melt, "*Who is this that cometh out of the wilderness like pillars of smoke, perfumed with myrrh and frankincense…?*" (Song of Solomon 3:6).

Thus does the soul ascend to God, by giving up self to the destroying and annihilating power of divine love. This is a state of sacrifice essential to the Christian religion, in which the soul suffers itself to be destroyed and annihilated so that it may pay homage to the sovereignty of God. As it is written, "*For great is the might of the Lord; he is glorified by the humble*" (Sirach 3:20 RSV). By the destruction of self, we acknowledge the supreme existence of God. We must cease to exist in self in order for the Spirit of the eternal Word to exist in us. It is by the giving up of our own lives that we give place to His coming, and in dying to ourselves, He Himself lives in us.

We must surrender our whole being to Christ Jesus and cease to live any longer in ourselves so that He may become our lives, that being dead, our lives may be hidden with Christ in God. (See Colossians 3:3.) God says to come to Him; but how is it that we come to Him? In no way but by leaving and forsaking ourselves so that we may be lost in Him, and this can be effected only by annihilation, which, being the true prayer of adoration, renders unto God alone all "*blessing, and honour, and glory, and power…for ever and ever*" (Revelation 5:13).

This is the prayer of truth; it is worshipping God in spirit and in truth. (See John 4:23.) We worship God in spirit by entering into the purity of the Spirit that prays within us, and by being drawn forth from our own carnal and human method. We worship in truth by being placed in the truth of the all of God and the nothing of the creature.

There are but these two truths, the all and the nothing; everything else is falsehood. We can pay due honor to the all of God only in our own annihilation, which is no sooner accomplished than He, who never allows a void in nature, instantly fills us with Himself.

Ah, did we but know the virtues and the blessings that the soul derives from this prayer, we should not be willing to do anything else. It is the pearl of great price, the hidden treasure (see Matthew 13:44–45), and whoever finds it sells freely all he has to purchase it; it is the well of living water that springs up to everlasting life (see John 4:14); it is the adoration of God *"in spirit and in truth"* (John 4:23); and it is the full performance of the purest evangelical precepts.

Jesus Christ assures us that *"the kingdom of God is within you"* (Luke 17:21), and this is true in two senses: First, when God becomes so fully Savior and Lord in us that nothing resists His domination, then our interior is His kingdom; second, when we possess God, who is the Supreme Good, we possess His kingdom also, wherein there is fullness of joy and where we attain the end of our creation. Thus it is said, "To serve God is to reign." The end of our creation, indeed, is to enjoy God, even in this life. But, alas, who thinks of it?

21

The Objections of Slothfulness and Inactivity

On the objections of slothfulness and inactivity made against this form of prayer (which are fully met), and on the truth that the soul acts nobly, forcibly, calmly, quickly, freely, simply, sweetly, temperately, and certainly (but in dependence upon God and moved by His Holy Spirit), because the restless and selfish activity of nature are being destroyed and the life of God communicated by union with Him.

Some persons, when they hear of the prayer of silence, falsely imagine that the soul remains stupid, dead, and inactive; but it unquestionably acts more nobly and more extensively than it has ever done before, for God Himself is its mover, and it now acts by the agency of His Spirit. Saint Paul would have us be led by the Spirit of God. (See Romans 8:14.)

It is not meant that we should cease from action but that we should act through the internal agency of His grace. This is finely represented by the prophet Ezekiel's vision of the wheels, which had a living Spirit, and wherever the Spirit was to go, they went. They ascended and descended as they were moved, and they returned not when they went. (See Ezekiel 1:19–21.) Thus the soul should be equally subservient to the will of that vivifying Spirit that is in it, and scrupulously faithful to follow only as the Spirit moves. These motions never tend to return in reflections on the creatures or self, but go forward in an incessant approach toward the end.

This activity of the soul is attended with the utmost tranquility. When it acts of itself, the act is forced and constrained, and therefore, it is more easily distinguished; but when the action is under the influence of the Spirit of grace, it is so free, so easy, and so natural that it almost seems as if we did not act at all. "*He brought me forth also into a large place; he delivered me, because he delighted in me*" (Psalm 18:19).

When the soul is in its central tendency, or, in other words, is returned through recollection into itself, from that moment, the central attraction becomes a most potent activity, infinitely surpassing in energy every other kind. Nothing, indeed, can equal the swiftness of this tendency to the center; and though an activity, it is yet so noble, so peaceful, so full of tranquility, so natural, and so spontaneous that it appears to the soul as if it was none at all.

When a wheel rolls slowly, we can easily perceive its parts, but when its motion is rapid, we can distinguish nothing. So the soul that rests in God has an activity exceedingly noble and elevated, yet altogether peaceful; and the more peaceful it is, the swifter is its course, because it is given up to that Spirit by which it is moved and directed.

This attracting Spirit is no one other than God Himself, who, in drawing us, causes us to run to Him. How well did the spouse understand this when she said, "*Draw me, we will run after thee*" (Song of Solomon 1:4). Draw me unto You, O my divine Center, by the secret springs of my existence, and all my powers and senses will follow You! This simple attraction is both an ointment to heal and a perfume to allure. "We follow," says she, "the fragrance of Your perfumes," and though so powerful an attraction, it is followed by the soul freely and without constraint. For it is equally delighted as forcible, and while it attracts by its power, it carries us away by its sweetness. *"Draw me,"* says the spouse, and *"we will run after thee"* (Song of Solomon 1:4). She speaks of herself and to herself: *"Draw me"*—behold the unity of the center that is drawn! *"We will run"*—behold the correspondence and course of all the senses and powers in following the attraction of the center!

Instead, then, of encouraging sloth, we promote the highest activity by inculcating a total dependence on the Spirit of God as our moving principle, for it is in Him and by Him alone that we live and move and have our being. (See Acts 17:28.) This meek dependence on the Spirit of God is indispensably necessary and causes the soul shortly to attain the unity and simplicity in which it was created.

We must, therefore, forsake our multifarious activity to enter into the simplicity and unity of God, in whose image we were originally formed. (See Genesis 1:27.) The Spirit is one and manifold (see Wisdom 7:22 RSV), and His unity does not preclude His multiplicity. We enter into His unity when we are united to His Spirit, and by that means, we have one and the same spirit with Him, and we are multiplied in respect to the outward execution of His will without any departure from our state of union.

In this way, when we are wholly moved by the divine Spirit, which is infinitely active, our activity must, indeed, be more energetic than that which is merely our own. We must yield ourselves to the guidance of wisdom, which *"is more mobile than any motion"* (Wisdom 7:24 RSV); and by abiding in dependence upon its action, our activity will be truly efficient.

"All things were made by him; and without him was not any thing made that was made" (John 1:3). God originally formed us in His own image and likeness. He breathed into us the Spirit of His Word—the breath of life that He gave to us at our creation (see Genesis 2:7) and in which the image of God consisted. Now this life is one, simple, pure, intimate, and always fruitful.

Since the devil broke and deformed the divine image in the soul by sin, the agency of the same Word whose Spirit was inbreathed at our creation is absolutely necessary for its renovation. It was necessary that it should be He, because He is the express image of His Father, and no image can be repaired by its own efforts, but must remain passive for that purpose under the hand of the workman.

Our activity should, therefore, consist in placing ourselves in a state of susceptibility to divine impressions and pliability to all the operations of the eternal Word. While tablet is unsteady, the painter is unable to produce a correct picture upon it, and every movement of self is productive of erroneous lineaments; it interrupts the work and defeats the design of this adorable Painter. We must then remain in peace, and move only when He moves us. Jesus Christ has life in Himself (see John 5:26), and He must give life to every living thing.

The spirit of the church of God is the spirit of the divine movement. Is she idle, barren, or unfruitful? No, she acts, but her activity is in dependence upon the Spirit of God, who moves and governs her. Just so should it be in her members; in order that they may be spiritual children of the church, they must be moved by the Spirit.

As all action is estimable only in proportion to the grandeur and dignity of the efficient principle, so this action is incontestably nobler than any other. Actions produced by a divine principle are *divine*; but creaturely actions, however good they appear, are only human, or at least virtuous, even when accompanied by grace.

Jesus Christ says that He has life in Himself. All other beings have only a borrowed life, but the Word has life in Himself, and being communicative of His nature, He desires to bestow it upon man. We should, therefore, make room for the influx of this life, which can only be done by the ejection and loss of the Adam life and the suppression of the activity of self. This is agreeable to an assertion of Saint Paul: "*If any man be in Christ, he is a new creature: old things are passed away; behold, all things are become new*" (2 Corinthians 5:17). But this state can be accomplished only by dying to ourselves and to all our own activity so that the activity of God may be substituted in its place.

Therefore, instead of prohibiting activity, we enjoin it, but in absolute dependence on the Spirit of God, that His activity may take the place of our own. This can be enacted only by the consent of the creature, and this concurrence can be yielded only by moderating our own action so that the activity of God may, little by little, be wholly substituted for it.

Jesus Christ has exemplified this in the gospels. Martha did what was right, but because she did it in her own spirit, Christ rebuked her. The spirit of man is restless and turbulent, for which reason he does little, though he seems to do a great deal. "*Martha,*" says Christ, "*thou art careful and troubled about many things: but one thing is needful: and Mary hath chosen that good part, which shall not be taken away from her*" (Luke 10:41–42). And what was it Mary had chosen? Repose, tranquility, and peace. She had apparently ceased to act so that the Spirit of Christ might act in her; she had ceased to live so that Christ might be her life.

This shows how necessary it is to renounce ourselves and all our activity to follow Christ, for we cannot follow Him if we are not animated by His Spirit. Now that His Spirit may gain admittance, it is necessary that our own should be expelled. Saint Paul says, "*He that is joined unto the Lord is one spirit*" (1 Corinthians 6:17). And David says it was good for him to draw near to the Lord and to put his trust in Him. (See Psalm 73:28.) What is this drawing near? It is the beginning of union.

Divine union has its commencement, its progress, its achievement, and its consummation. It is at first an inclination toward

God. When the soul is introverted in the manner before described, it gets within the influence of the central attraction, and acquires an eager desire after union. This is only the beginning. It then adheres to Him when it has gotten nearer and nearer, and it finally becomes one, that is, one spirit with Him. Then it is that the spirit that had wandered from God returns again to its end.

Into this way, then, which is the divine motion and the spirit of Jesus Christ, we must necessarily enter. Saint Paul says, "*If any man have not the Spirit of Christ, he is none of his*" (Romans 8:9). Therefore, to be Christ's, we must be filled with His Spirit and emptied of our own. The apostle, in the same chapter, proved the necessity of this divine influence. He says, "*As many as are led by the Spirit of God, they are the sons of God*" (Romans 8:14).

The spirit of divine filiation is, then, the spirit of divine motion. Paul therefore adds, "*Ye have not received the spirit of bondage again to fear; but ye have received the Spirit of adoption, whereby we cry, Abba, Father*" (Romans 8:15). This spirit is none other than the Spirit of Christ, through which we participate in His filiation. "*The Spirit itself beareth witness with our spirit, that we are the children of God*" (Romans 8:16).

When the soul yields itself to the influence of this blessed Spirit, it perceives the testimony of its divine filiation, and it feels also, with superadded joy, that it has received, not the spirit of bondage, but the spirit of liberty, even the liberty of the children of God. It then finds that it acts freely and sweetly, though with vigor and infallibility.

The spirit of divine action is so necessary in all things that Saint Paul, in the same passage, bases that necessity on our ignorance with respect to what we pray for. He says, "*The Spirit also helpeth our infirmities: for we know not what we should pray for as we ought: but the Spirit itself maketh intercession for us with groanings which cannot be uttered*" (Romans 8:26). This is plain enough; if we know not what we stand in need of or how to pray as we ought for those things that are necessary, and if the Spirit that is in us and to which we resign ourselves must ask for us, should we not permit Him to give vent to His unutterable groanings on our behalf?

This Spirit is the Spirit of the Word, which is always heard, as He says Himself: *"I knew that thou hearest me always"* (John 11:42), and if we freely admit this Spirit to pray and intercede for us, we also will always be eard. And why? We learn from the same great apostle, the skillful mystic and master of the interior life, that *"He that searcheth the hearts knoweth what is the mind of the Spirit, because he maketh intercession for the saints according to the will of God"* (Romans 8:27). That is to say, the Spirit demands only what is conformable to the will of God. The will of God is that we should be saved and that we should become perfect. He, therefore, intercedes for all that is necessary for our perfection.

Why, then, should we be burdened with superfluous cares and weary ourselves in the multiplicity of our ways without ever saying, "Let us rest in peace"? God Himself invites us to cast all our cares upon Him, and He complains in Isaiah, with ineffable goodness, that the soul had expended its powers and its treasures on a thousand external objects when there was so little to do to attain all it need desire. *"Wherefore,"* says God, *"do ye spend money for that which is not bread? and your labour for that which satisfieth not? Hearken diligently unto me, and eat ye that which is good, and let your soul delight itself in fatness"* (Isaiah 55:2).

Oh, if only we knew the blessedness of listening to God in this, and how greatly the soul is strengthened by such a course! *"Be silent, O all flesh, before the Lord"* (Zechariah 2:13); all must cease as soon as He appears. But to engage us still further to abandonment without reservation, God assures us, by the same prophet, that we need fear nothing because He takes very special care of us. *"Can a woman forget her sucking child, that she should not have compassion on the son of her womb? Yea, she may forget, yet will I not forget thee*" (Isaiah 49:15). O words full of consolation! Who, after that, will fear to abandon himself wholly to the guidance of God?

22

The Distinction Between Inward and Outward Acts

On the distinction between inward and outward acts—in this state the acts of the soul are inward, but habitual, continued, direct, lasting, deep, simple, unconscious, and resembling a gentle and perpetual sinking into the ocean of divinity—and on a comparison and how to act when we perceive no attraction.

We have both external and internal actions. External acts are those that appear outwardly, bear relation to some sensible object, and have no moral character, except such as they derive from the principle from which they proceed. I intend here to speak only of internal acts, those energies of the soul by which it turns toward some objects and away from other objects.

If during my application to God I should form a will to change the nature of my act, I should thereby withdraw myself from God and turn to created objects, and that in a greater or lesser degree according to the strength of the act. And if, when I am turned toward the creature, I would return to God, I must necessarily form an act for that purpose; and the more perfect this act is, the more complete is the conversion.

Till conversion is perfected, many reiterated acts are necessary, for it is progressive with some, although instantaneous with others. My act, however, should consist in a continual turning to God, an exertion of every faculty and power of the soul purely for Him, agreeably to the instructions of the son of Sirach, "Reunite all the motions of thy heart in the holiness of God," and to the example of David, *"Because of his strength will I wait upon thee: for God is my defence"* (Psalm 59:9). For we have strayed from our heart by sinning, and it is our heart only that God requires of us: *"My son give me thine heart, and let thine eyes observe my ways"* (Proverbs 23:26). To give our hearts to God is to have the whole energy of our souls ever centered in Him, so that we may be rendered conformable to His will. We must, therefore, continue invariably turned to God from our first application to Him.

But the spirit is unstable, and the soul is accustomed to turn to external objects; it is easily distracted. This evil, however, will be counteracted if, on perceiving the wandering, we, by a pure act of returning to God, instantly replace ourselves in Him. And this act subsists as long as the conversion lasts, by the powerful influence of a simple and unfeigned return to God.

As many reiterated acts form a habit, the soul contracts the habit of conversion, and that act that was before interrupted and distinct becomes habitual.

The soul should not, then, be perplexed about forming an act that already subsists, and that, indeed, it cannot attempt to form without very great difficulty. It even finds that it is withdrawn from its proper state, under pretence of seeking that which is in reality acquired, seeing the habit is already formed; and it is confirmed in habitual conversion and habitual love. It is seeking one act by the help of many, instead of continuing attached to God by one simple act alone.

We may remark that at times we form with facility many distant yet simple acts, which shows that we have wandered and that we re-enter our heart after having strayed from it. Yet when we have re-entered, we should remain there in peace. We err, therefore, in supposing that we must not form acts. We form them continually, but let them be conformable to the degree of our spiritual advancement.

The great difficulty with most spiritual people arises from their lack of clear comprehension of this matter. Now, some acts are transient and distinct, while others are continued; further, some are direct and others reflective. All cannot form the first; neither are all in a state suited to form the others. The first are adapted to those who have strayed and who require a distinct exertion, proportioned to the extent of their deviation. If the latter be inconsiderable, an act of the simplest kind is sufficient.

By the *continued* act, I mean that whereby the soul is altogether turned toward God by a direct act, always subsisting, and that it does not renew unless it has been interrupted. The soul, being thus turned, is in charity and abides therein: *"And he that dwelleth in love dwelleth in God"* (1 John 4:16). The soul, then, as it were, exists and rests in the habitual act. It is, however, free from sloth, for there is still an uninterrupted act subsisting, which is a sweet sinking into the Deity, whose attraction becomes more and more powerful. Following this potent attraction and dwelling in love and charity, the soul sinks continually deeper into that love, maintaining an activity infinitely more powerful, vigorous, and effectual than that which served to accomplish its first return.

Now the soul that is thus profoundly and vigorously active, being wholly given up to God, does not perceive this act, because it is direct and unreflective. This is the reason why some, not expressing themselves properly, say that they make no acts, but it is a mistake, for they were never more truly or nobly active. They should say that they did not distinguish their acts, not that they did not act. I grant that they do not act in themselves, but they are drawn, and they follow the attraction. Love is the weight that sinks them. As one falling into the sea would sink from one depth to another to all eternity, if the sea were infinite, so they, without perceiving their descent, drop with inconceivable swiftness into the lowest depths.

It is, then, improper to say that we do not make acts; all form acts, but the manner of their formation is not alike in all. The mistake arises from this, that all who know they should act are desirous of acting distinguishably and perceptibly, but this cannot be. Sensible acts are for beginners; there are others for those in a more advanced state. To stop the former sensible acts, which are weak and of little profit, is to declare ourselves of the latter. To attempt the latter without having passed through the former is a no less considerable error.

"To every thing there is a season" (Ecclesiastes 3:1). Every state has its commencement, its progress, and its consummation, and it is an unhappy error to stop in the beginning. There is no art but what has its progress; at first we labor with toil, but at last we reap the fruit of our industry.

When the vessel is in port, the mariners are obliged to exert all their strength so that they may clear her thence and put to sea, but they subsequently turn her with facility as they please. In like manner, while the soul remains in sin and the creature, many endeavors are requisite to effect its freedom. The cables that hold it must be loosed, and then, by strong and vigorous efforts, it gathers itself inward, pushes off gradually from the old port of self, and leaving that behind, proceeds to the interior, the haven so much desired.

When the vessel is thus started, as she advances on the sea, she leaves the shore behind, and the farther she departs from the land, the less labor is requisite in moving her forward. At length she begins to get gently under sail and now proceeds so swiftly in her course that the oars, which have become useless, are laid aside.

How is the pilot now employed? He is content with spreading the sails and holding the rudder.

To "spread the sails" is to lay ourselves before God in the prayer of simple exposition, to be moved by His Spirit. To "hold the rudder" is to restrain our heart from wandering from the true course, recalling it gently and guiding it steadily by the dictates of the Spirit of God, which gradually gain possession of the heart, just as the breeze by degrees fills the sails and impels the vessel. While the winds are fair, the pilot and the mariners rest from their labors. What progress they now secure without the least fatigue! They make more way now in one hour, while they rest and leave the vessel to the wind, than they did in a length of time by all their former efforts. And even if they were now to attempt using the oars, besides greatly fatiguing themselves, they would only retard the vessel by their useless exertions.

This is our proper course interiorly, and a short time will advance us by the divine impulsion farther than many reiterated acts of self-exertion. Whoever will try this path will find it the easiest in the world.

If the wind be contrary and blow a storm, we must cast anchor in the sea to hold the vessel. This anchor is simply trust in God and hope in His goodness, waiting patiently for the calming of the tempest and the return of a favorable gale. Thus did David: *"I waited patiently for the Lord; and he inclined unto me, and heard my cry"* (Psalm 40:1). We must, therefore, be resigned to the Spirit of God, wholly giving ourselves up to His divine guidance.

23

The Barrenness of Evils from Lack of Prayer

On the barrenness of preaching, vice, error, heresies, and all sorts of evils arising from the fact that people are not instructed in the prayer of the heart (although the way is surer, easier, and fitter for the simpleminded); and an exhortation to pastors to set their flocks upon the practice of it without employing them in studied forms and methodical devotion.

If all who labored for the conversion of others sought to reach them by the heart, introducing them immediately to prayer and the interior life, numberless and permanent conversions would ensue. On the contrary, few and transient fruits must attend that labor that is confined to outward matters, such as burdening the disciple with a thousand precepts for external exercises instead of leading the soul to Christ by the occupation of the heart in Him.

If ministers were solicitous thus to instruct their parishioners, shepherds, while they watched their flocks, would have the spirit of the primitive Christians; the husbandman at the plough would maintain a blessed communion with his Go; the manufacturer, while he exhausted his outward man with labor, would be renewed with inward strength; every kind of vice would shortly disappear; and every parishioner would become spiritually minded.

O when once the heart is gained, how easily is all the rest corrected! This is why God, above all things, requires the heart. By this means alone, we may extirpate the dreadful vices that so prevail among the lower orders, such as drunkenness, blasphemy, lewdness, enmity, and theft. Jesus Christ would reign everywhere in peace, and the face of the church would be renewed throughout.

The decay of internal piety is unquestionably the source of the various errors that have appeared in the world; all would speedily be overthrown if inward devotion was re-established. Errors take possession of no soul except those that are deficient in faith and prayer, and if, instead of engaging our wandering brethren in constant disputations, we would but teach them simply to believe and diligently to pray, we would lead them sweetly to God.

O how inexpressibly great is the loss sustained by mankind from the neglect of the interior life! And what an account will need to be given by who are entrusted with the care of souls and have not discovered and communicated to their flock this hidden treasure!

Some excuse themselves by saying that there is danger in this way or that simple persons are incapable of comprehending the things of the Spirit. But the oracles of truth affirm the contrary: "*They that deal truly are* [God's] *delight*" (Proverbs 12:22). But what danger can there be in walking in the only true way, which is Jesus Christ, giving ourselves up to Him, fixing our eye continually on Him, placing all our confidence in His grace, and tending with all the strength of our soul to His purest love?

The simple ones, so far from being incapable of this perfection, are by their docility, innocence, and humility peculiarly qualified for its attainment; and as they are not accustomed to reasoning, they are less tenacious of their own opinions. Even from their want of learning, they submit more freely to the teachings of the divine Spirit. By contrast, others who are cramped and blinded by self-sufficiency offer much greater resistance to the operations of grace.

We are told in Scripture that "*the entrance of* [God's] *words giveth...understanding unto the simple*" (Psalm 119:130), and we are also assured that God loves to communicate with the simple-minded: "*The* Lord *preserveth the simple: I was brought low, and he helped me*" (Psalm 116:6). Let spiritual fathers be careful how they prevent their little ones from coming to Christ. He Himself said to His apostles, "*Suffer little children...to come unto me, for of such is the kingdom of heaven*" (Matthew 19:14). It was the endeavor of the apostles to prevent children from going to our Lord that occasioned this command.

Man frequently applies a remedy to the outward body while the disease lies at the heart. The cause of our lack of success in reforming mankind, especially those of the lower classes, is that we begin with external matters. All our labors in this field produce fruit that does not endure, but if the key of the interior be first given, the exterior would be naturally and easily reformed.

Now this is very easy. To teach man to seek God in His heart, to think of Him, to return to Him whenever he finds he has wandered from Him, and to do and to suffer all things with a single eye to please Him, is leading the soul to the source of all grace and causing it to find there everything necessary for sanctification.

I, therefore, beseech you all, O you who have the care of souls, to put them at once into this way, which is Jesus Christ. No, it is He Himself who conjures you, by all the blood He has shed for those entrusted to you. "*Speak ye comfortably to Jerusalem*" (Isaiah 40:2). O you dispensers of His grace, preachers of His word, ministers of His sacraments, establish His kingdom! And that it may indeed be established, make Him ruler over the heart! For as it is the heart alone that can oppose His sovereignty, it is by the subjection of the heart that His sovereignty is most highly honored: "*Sanctify the* Lord *of hosts himself; and let him be your fear....And he shall be for a sanctuary*" (Isaiah 8:13). Compose catechisms expressly to teach prayer, not by reasoning or by methods, for the simple are incapable of that, but teach the prayer of the heart, not of understanding—the prayer of God's Spirit, not of man's invention.

Alas, by directing them to pray in elaborate forms and to be curiously critical therein, you create their chief obstacles. The children have been led astray from the best of fathers by your endeavoring to teach them too refined a language. Go, then, you poor children, to your heavenly Father. Speak to Him in your natural language, rude and barbarous as it may be; it is not so to Him. A father is better pleased with an address that love and respect have made confused—because He sees that it proceeds from the heart—than He is by a dry and barren harangue, though ever so elaborate. The simple and undisguised emotions of love are infinitely more expressive than all language and all reasoning.

Men have desired to love love by formal rules, and have thus lost much of that love. O how unnecessary is it to teach an art of loving! The language of love is barbarous to him who does not love, but perfectly natural to him who does, and there is no better way to learn how to love God than to love Him. The most ignorant often become the most perfect, because they proceed with more cordiality and simplicity. The Spirit of God needs none of our arrangements. When it pleases Him, He turns shepherds into prophets, and so far from excluding any from the temple of prayer, He throws wide the gates that all may enter. Wisdom is directed to cry aloud in the highways, "*Whoso is simple, let him turn in hither*" (Proverbs 9:4), and to the fools she says, "*Come, eat of my bread, and drink of the wine which I have mingled*" (Proverbs 9:5). And does not Jesus Christ Himself thank His Father for having "*hid these things from the wise and prudent, and hast revealed them unto babes*" (Matthew 11:25)?

24

THE PASSIVE WAY TO DIVINE UNION

On the passive way to divine union.

It is impossible to attain divine union solely by the way of meditation or of the affections or by any devotion, no matter how illuminated. There are many reasons for this, the chief of which are those that follow.

According to Scripture, no man will see God and live. (See Exodus 33:20.) Now all the exercises of discursive prayer and even of active contemplation, regarded as an end and not as a mere preparative to that which is passive, are still living exercises by which we cannot see God. That is to say, be united with Him. All that is of man and of his doing, no matter how noble or exalted, must first be destroyed.

Saint John relates that there was silence in heaven. (See Revelation 8:1.) Now heaven represents the ground and center of the soul, wherein all must be hushed to silence when the majesty of God appears. All the efforts, nay, the very existence of self, must be destroyed, because nothing is opposite to God but self, and all the malignity of man is in self-appropriation as the source of its evil nature. The purity of a soul increases in proportion to the extent it loses this selfhood. And the things that were faults while the soul lived in self-appropriation are no longer such after it has acquired purity and innocence by departing from that selfhood, which caused the dissimilitude between it and God.

To unite two things so opposite as the purity of God and the impurity of the creature, the simplicity of God and the multiplicity of man, much more is requisite than the efforts of the creature. Nothing less than an efficacious operation of the Almighty can ever accomplish this, for two things must have some relation or similarity before they can become one, as the impurity of dross cannot be united with the purity of gold.

What, then, does God do? He sends His own wisdom before Him, as fire will be sent upon the earth to destroy by its activity all that is impure. As nothing can resist the power of that fire, consuming everything, so too this wisdom destroys all the impurities of the creature in order to dispose it for divine union.

The impurity that is so fatal to union consists in self-appropriation and activity. Self-appropriation is the source and fountain of all that defilement that can never be allied to essential purity—as the rays of the sun may shine, indeed, upon mire, but can never be united with it. And since God is in an infinite stillness, the soul, in order to be united to Him, must participate of His stillness; otherwise, the contrariety between stillness and activity would prevent assimilation.

Therefore, the soul can never arrive at divine union but in the rest of its will; nor can it ever become one with God but by being re-established in central rest and in the purity of its first creation.

God purifies the soul by His wisdom as refiners do metals in the furnace. Gold cannot be purified but by fire, which gradually consumes all that is earthy and foreign and separates it from the metal. It is not sufficient to fit it for use that the earthy part should be changed into gold; it must then be melted and dissolved by the force of fire to separate from the mass every drossy or alien particle, and it must be again and again cast into the furnace until it has lost every trace of pollution and every possibility of being further purified.

The goldsmith cannot now discover any adulterate mixture because of its perfect purity and simplicity. The fire no longer touches it, and if it remained an age in the furnace, its spotlessness would not be increased or its substance diminished. It is then fit for the most exquisite workmanship, and if, thereafter, this gold seems obscured or defiled, it is nothing more than an accidental impurity occasioned by the contact of some foreign body and is only superficial. It is no hindrance to its employment, and is widely different from its former debasement, which was hidden in the ground of its nature and, as it were, identified with it. Those, however, who are uninstructed, beholding the pure gold sullied by some external pollution, would be disposed to prefer an impure and gross metal that appeared superficially bright and polished.[8]

Further, the pure and the impure gold are not mingled. Before they can be united, they must be equally refined; the goldsmith cannot mix dross and gold. What will he do, then? He will purge out the dross with fire so that the inferior may become as pure as the other, and then they may be united. This is what Saint Paul means when he declares that *"the fire shall try every man's work of what sort it is"* (1 Corinthians 3:13); he adds, *"If any man's work be burned, he shall suffer loss: but he himself shall be saved; yet so as by fire"* (1 Corinthians 3:15). He here intimates that there are works so degraded by impure mixtures that, though the mercy of God accepts them, they must

8. "God knows that (in speaking of the superficial impurity) I had only reference to certain defects which are exterior and entirely natural, and which are left by God in the greatest saints to keep them from pride, and the sight of men, who judge only from the outward appearance, to preserve them from corruption, and hide them in the secret of his presence. (Ps. mod. 20.) At the time I wrote, I had heard no mention of the perversions subsequently spoken of that those in union with God might sin and yet remain united to Him, and, as such an idea had not once occurred to me, I never imagined that it was possible for anyone to draw such inferences from a simple illustration." —Madame Guyon, *Courte Apologie*

pass through the fire to be purged from self. It is in this sense that God is said to examine and judge our righteousness, because by the deeds of the law, no flesh will be justified, but only by the righteousness of God, which is by faith in Jesus Christ. (See Romans 3:20.)

Thus we may see that the divine justice and wisdom, like a pitiless and devouring fire, must destroy all that is earthly, sensual, and carnal, as well as all self-activity, before the soul can be united to its God. Now this can never be accomplished by the industry of the creature; on the contrary, he always submits to it with reluctance, because, as I have said, he is so enamored of self and so fearful of its destruction that if God did not act upon him powerfully and with authority, he would never consent.

It may, perhaps, be objected here that as God never robs man of his free will, he can always resist the divine operations, and that I, therefore, err in saying God acts absolutely, and without the consent of man.

Let me, however, explain. By man's giving a passive consent, God, without usurpation, may assume full power and an entire guidance; for having, in the beginning of his conversion, made an unreserved surrender of himself to all that God wills of him or by him, he thereby gave an active consent to whatever God might afterward require. But when God begins to burn, destroy, and purify, the soul does not perceive that these operations are intended for its good, but rather supposes the contrary. And as the gold at first seems rather to blacken than brighten in the fire, so it conceives that its purity is lost—so much so that if an active and explicit consent were then required, the soul could scarcely give it and would often withhold it. All it does is to remain firm in its passive consent, enduring as patiently as possible all these divine operations that it is neither able nor desirous to obstruct.

In this manner, therefore, the soul is purified from all its self-originated, distinct, perceptible, and multiplied operations, which constitute a great dissimilitude between it and God. It is rendered by degrees "conform," and then "uniform," and the passive capacity of the creature is elevated, ennobled, and enlarged, though in a secret and hidden manner, hence called mystical. But in all these operations, the soul must concur passively. It is true, indeed, that in the beginning, its activity is requisite; however, as the divine operations become stronger, it must gradually cease from them, yielding itself up to the impulse of the divine Spirit, till it is wholly absorbed in Him. But this is a process that lasts a long time.

We do not, then, say, as some have supposed, that there is no need of activity, since on the contrary, it is the gate. However, we should not always tarry at it since we ought to tend toward ultimate perfection, which is impracticable except if the first helps are laid aside. For however necessary they may have been at the entrance of the road, they afterward become greatly detrimental to those who adhere to them obstinately, preventing them from ever attaining the end. This made Saint Paul say, *"Forgetting those things which are behind, and reaching forth unto those things which are before, I press toward the mark for the prize of the high calling of God in Christ Jesus"* (Philippians 3:13–14).

Would you not say that he had lost his senses, who, having undertaken a journey, should fix his abode at the first inn because he had been told that many travelers had come that way, that some had lodged there, and that the masters of the house dwelt there? All that we wish, then, is that souls would press toward the end, taking the shortest and easiest road and not stopping at the first stage. Let them follow the counsel and example of Saint Paul and allow themselves to be led by the Spirit of God (see Romans 8:14), who will infallibly conduct them to the end of their creation, the enjoyment of God.

But while we confess that the enjoyment of God is the end for which alone we were created, and that every soul that does not attain divine union and the purity of its creation in this life can only be saved as by fire, how strange it is that we should dread and avoid the process—as if that which is to produce the perfection of glory in the life to come could be the cause of evil and imperfection in the present life.

None can be ignorant that God is the Supreme Good, that essential blessedness consists in union with Him, that the saints differ in glory depending on whether their union is more or less perfect, and that the soul cannot attain this union by the mere activity of its own powers, since God communicates Himself to the soul in proportion to its passive capacity to be great, noble, and extensive. We can only be united to God in simplicity and passivity, and as this union is beatitude itself, the way that leads us in this passivity cannot be evil but must be the most free from danger and the best.

This way is not dangerous. Would Jesus Christ have made this the most perfect and necessary of all ways, had it been so? No! All can travel it, and as all are called to happiness, all are likewise called to the enjoyment of God, both in this life and in the next, for that alone is happiness. I say the enjoyment of God Himself, and not of His gifts. These latter do not constitute essential beatitude, as they cannot fully content the soul. It is so noble and so great that the most exalted gifts of God cannot make it happy unless the Giver also bestows Himself. Now the whole desire of the Divine Being is to give Himself to every creature according to the capacity with which it is endowed. And yet, alas, how reluctantly man suffers himself to be drawn to God! How fearful he is to prepare for divine union!

Some say that we must not place ourselves in this state. I grant it, but I say also that no creature could ever do it, since it would not be possible for any, by all their own efforts, to unite themselves to God. It is He alone who must do it. It is altogether idle, then, to exclaim against those who are self-united, as such a thing cannot be.

They say again that some may feign to have attained this state. None can any more feign this than the wretch who is on the point of perishing with hunger can, for any length of time at least, feign to be full and satisfied. Some wish or word, some sigh or sign, will inevitably escape him and betray that he is far from being satisfied.

Since then none can attain this end by their own labor, we do not pretend to introduce any into it, but only to point out the way that leads to it—beseeching all not to become attached to the accommodations on the road, the external practices, which must all be left behind when the signal is given. The experienced instructor knows this, points to the water of life, and lends his aid to obtain it. Would it not be an unjustifiable cruelty to show a spring to a thirsty man and then bind him so that he could not reach it and cause him to die of thirst?

This is just what is done every day. Let us all agree in the way, as we all agree in the end, which is evident and incontrovertible. The way has its beginning, process, and termination, and the nearer we approach the consummation, the farther is the beginning behind us. It is only by leaving the one that we can arrive at the other. You cannot get from the entrance to a distant place without passing over the intermediate space, and if the end be good, holy, and necessary, and the entrance also good, why should the necessary passage, the direct road leading from the one to the other, be evil?

O the blindness of the greater part of mankind, who pride themselves on science and wisdom! How true is it, O my God, that You have hidden these things from the wise and prudent and have revealed them unto babes! (See Matthew 11:25.)

On the Way to God

By Madame Guyon

A concise view of the way to God and the state of union.

"And the glory which thou gavest me I have given them; that they may be one, even as we are one: I in them, and thou in me, that they may be made perfect in one."

—John 17:22–23

CONTENTS

Part I:
On the Way to God

1

The First Degree: Conversion

The first degree is the return of the soul to God, when, being truly converted, it begins to subsist by means of grace.

2

The Second Degree: The Effectual Touch in the Will

The soul then receives an effectual touch in the will, which invites it to recollection and instructs it that God is within and must be sought there, that He is present in the heart and must be there enjoyed.

In the beginning, this discovery is the source of very great joy to the soul, as it is an intimation or pledge of happiness to come; in its very commencement, the road it is to pursue is opened and is shown to be that of the inward life. This knowledge is the more admirable, as it is the spring of all the felicity of the soul and the solid foundation of interior progress, for those souls who tend toward God merely by the intellect, even though they should enjoy a somewhat spiritual contemplation, can never enter into intimate union if they do not quit that path and enter this of the inward touch, where the whole working is in the will.

Those who are led in this way, though conducted by a blind abandonment, experience a savory knowledge. They never walk by the light of the intellect like the former, who receive distinct lights to guide them and who, having a clear view of the road, never enter those impenetrable passes of the hidden will that are reserved for the latter. The former proceed upon the evidence furnished by their illuminations and assisted by their reason, and they do well. But the latter are destined to pursue blindly an unknown course, which, nevertheless, appears perfectly natural to them, although they seem obliged to feel their way. They go, however, with more certainty than the others, who are subject to be misled in their intellectual illuminations. But these are guided by a supreme Will that conducts them howsoever it will. And further, all the more immediate operations are performed in the center of the soul, that is, in the three powers reduced to the unity of the will, where they are all absorbed, insensibly following the path prescribed for them by that touch to which we have before referred.

These latter are those who pursue the way of faith and absolute abandonment. They have neither relish nor liberty for any other path; all else constrains and embarrasses them. They dwell in greater dryness than the others, for as there is nothing distinct to which their minds are attached, their thoughts often wander and have nothing to fix them. And there are differences in souls; some have more sensible delights, and others have drier ones. So it is with those who are led by the will; the former sort have more relish and less solid acquirement and should restrain their too eager disposition and suffer their emotions to pass, even when they seem burning with love. The latter seem harder and more insensible, and their state appears altogether natural; nevertheless, there is a delicate something in the depth of the will that serves to nourish them, and that is, as it were, the condensed essence of what the others experience in the intellect and in ardor of purpose.

Still, as this support is exceedingly delicate, it frequently becomes imperceptible and is hidden by the slightest thing. This gives rise to great suffering, especially in times of tribulation and temptation, for as the relish and support are delicate and concealed, the will partakes of the same character in a high degree so that such souls have none of those strong wills. Their state is more indifferent and insensible, and their way more equable. But this does not hinder them from having a severe and even more serious trouble than others, for nothing being done in them by impulse, everything takes place, as it were, naturally; and their feeble, insensible, hidden wills cannot be found to make head against their foes. Their fidelity, however, often excels that of the others. Notice the striking difference between Peter and John. One seems to be overflowing with extraordinary zeal and falls away at the voice of a maidservant; the other makes no external manifestation and remains faithful unto the end.

You will ask me, then, if these souls that are urged on by no violent influence, but walk in blindness, do the will of God. They do, more truly, although they have no distinct assurance of it. His will is engraved in indelible characters on their very inmost recesses, so that they perform with a cold and languid, but firm and inviolable, abandonment, what the others accomplish by the drawings of an exquisite delight.

Thus they go on under the influence of this divine touch, from one degree to another, by a faith more or less sensibly savory, and they experience constant alternations of dryness and enjoyment of the presence of God, but ever finding that the enjoyment becomes continually deeper and less perceptible and thus more delicate and interior. They discover, too, that in the midst of their dryness, and without any distinct illumination, they are not the less enlightened. For this state is luminous in itself, though dark to the soul that dwells in it. And so true is this that they find themselves more acquainted with the truth. I mean that truth implanted in their interior, which causes everything to yield to the will of God. This divine will becomes more familiar to them, and they are enabled, in their insipid way, to penetrate a thousand mysteries that never could have been discovered by the light of reason and knowledge. They are insensibly and gradually preparing, without being aware of it, for the states that are to follow.

The trials of this state are alternations of dryness and facility. The former purified the attachment or tendency and natural relish that we have for the enjoyment of God. The whole of this degree is passed in these alternations of enjoyment, dryness, and facility, without any intermixture of temptations, except very transitory ones, or certain faults. For in every state, from the beginning onward, the faults of nature are much more liable to overtake us in times of dryness than in seasons of interior joy, when the unction of grace secures us from a thousand evils. In all the preceding states thus far, the soul is engaged in combating its evil habits and in endeavoring to overcome them by all sorts of painful self-denial.

In the beginning, when God turned the soul's look inward, He so influenced it against itself that it was obliged to cut off all its enjoyments, even the most innocent, and to load itself with every kind of affliction. God gives no respite to some in this regard, until the life of nature—that is, of the exterior senses as manifested in appetites, likes, and dislikes—is wholly destroyed.

This destruction of the appetites and repugnance of the outward senses belongs to the second degree, which I have called the effectual touch in the will and in which the highest and greatest virtue is practiced, especially when the inward drawing is vigorous and the unction very savory. For there is no sort of contrivance that God does not discover to the soul to enable it to conquer and overcome self in everything, so that, at length, by this constant practice, accompanied by the gracious unction before referred to, the spirit gets the upper hand of nature, and the interior part comes under subjection without resistance. There is, then, no further trouble from this source, any more than if all external feeling had been taken away. This state is mistaken for a state of death by those who are but little enlightened; it is, indeed, the death of the senses, but there is yet a long way to that of the spirit.

3

The Third Degree: Passivity and Interior Sacrifice

When we have for some time enjoyed the repose of a victory that has cost us so much trouble and suppose ourselves forever relieved from an enemy whose whole power has been destroyed, we enter into the third degree, next in order to the other, which is a way of faith more or less savory, according to the state. We enter into a condition of alternate dryness and facility, as I have stated, and in this dryness, the soul perceives certain exterior weaknesses, natural defects that, though slight, take it by surprise. It feels, too, that the strength it had received for the struggle is dying away. This is caused by the loss of our active, inward force. For although the soul, in the second degree, imagines itself to be in silence before God, it is not entirely so. It does not speak, indeed, either in heart or by mouth, but it is in an active striving after God and constant outbreathing of love so that, as the subject of the most powerful amorous activity exerted by the divine love toward Himself, it is continually leaping, as it were, toward its object, and its activity is accompanied by a delightful and almost constant peace. As it is from this activity of love that we acquire the strength to overcome nature, it is then that we practice the greatest virtues and most severe mortifications.

But just in proportion to how this activity decays and is lost in an amorous passivity, so does our strength of resistance sink and diminish; and as this degree advances and the soul becomes more and more passive, it becomes more and more powerless in combat. As God becomes strong within, so do we become weak. Some regard this impossibility of resistance as a great temptation, but they do not see that all our labor, aided and assisted by grace, can only accomplish the conquest of our outward senses, after which God takes gradual possession of our interior and becomes Himself our purifier. And as He required all our watchfulness while He continued us in amorous activity, so He now requires all our fidelity to let Him work while He begins to render Himself Lord by the subjection of the flesh to the Spirit.

For it must be observed that all our outward perfection depends upon and must follow the inward, so that when we are employed in active devotion, however simple, we are actively engaged against ourselves just as simply.

The second degree accomplishes the destruction of the outward senses; the third, that of the inward, and this is brought about by means of this savory passivity. But as God is then working within, He seems to neglect the outward, and hence the reappearance of defects, though feebly and only in a time of aridity, that we thought extinct.

The nearer we approach the termination of the third degree, the longer and more frequent are our dry seasons, and the greater our weakness. This is a purification that serves to destroy our internal feelings, as the amorous activity put an end to our external; and in each degree, there are alternations of dryness and enjoyment. The dryness serves as a purifier from its barrenness and weakness. As soon as we cease from inability to practice mortifications of our own fashioning, those of Providence take their place—the crosses that God dispenses according to our degree. These are not chosen by the soul, but the soul, under the interior guidance of God, receives such as He appoints.

4

The Fourth Degree: Naked Faith

The fourth degree is naked faith; here we have nothing but inward and outward desolation, for the one always follows the other.

Every degree has its beginning, progress, and consummation.

All that has hitherto been granted and acquired with so much labor is here gradually taken away.

This degree is the longest and only ends with total death, if the soul be willing to be so desolated as to die wholly to self. For there is an infinite number of souls who never pass the first degrees, and of those who reach the present state, there are very few in whom its perfect work is accomplished.

This desolation takes place in some with violence, and although they suffer more distress than others, they have less reason to complain, for the very severity of their affliction is a sort of consolation. There are others who experience only a feebleness and a kind of disgust for everything, which has the appearance of being a failure in duty and unwillingness to obey.

We are first deprived of our voluntary works and become unable to do what we did in the preceding degrees, and as this increases, we begin to feel a general inability in respect to everything that, instead of diminishing, enlarges day by day. As this weakness and inability gradually takes possession of us, we enter upon a condition in which we say, "*For that which I do I allow not: for what I would, that do I not; but what I hate, that do I*" (Romans 7:15).

After being thus deprived of all things, both inward and outward, that are not essential, the work begins upon those who are. In proportion to the disappearance of the virtuous life of becoming a Christian, which we regarded with so much complacency, we are likewise spoiled of a certain interior delight and substantial support.[9] As this support becomes weaker and more subtle, the more perceptible becomes its loss. It is to be remarked, however, that there is no loss except to our own consciousness, as it still exists in the soul, but imperceptibly and without apparent action. If it were not hidden, the death and loss of self could not be accomplished. But it retires within and shuts itself up so closely that the soul is not aware of its presence.

Do you ask why this course is pursued? The whole object of the way thus far has been to cause the soul to pass from multiplicity to the distinct sensible without multiplicity; from the distinct sensible to the distinct insensible; then to the sensible indistinct, which is a general delight much less attractive than the other. It is vigorous in the beginning and introduces the soul into the perceived, which is a purer and less exquisite pleasure than the first. Then from the perceived it moves into faith sustained and working by love, passing in this way from the sensible to the spiritual and from the spiritual to naked faith, which, causing us to be dead to all spiritual experiences, makes us die to ourselves and pass into God so that we may live henceforth from the life of God only.

9. Note from the editor: It is not at all likely that anyone who has attentively read thus far in this little work will suppose that when the "virtuous life of becoming a Christian" is said to disappear, it is meant that the person in this state is suffered to fall away into open sin. It simply disappears from his own eyes; to those of others, as well as to God, he exhibits in his degree, as ever, the Lord Jesus.

In the economy of grace, then, we begin with sensible things, continue with those that are spiritual, and end by leading the soul gradually into its center and uniting it with God.

The more deeply this imperceptible support retires, the more does it knit the soul together so that it cannot continue to multiply itself among a thousand things that it can no longer either affect or even perceive; and entirely stripped, it is gradually obliged to desert even itself.

It is stripped without mercy, then, equally and at the same time, of everything both within and without, and what is worst of all is delivered over to temptations, and the more fully it is thus given up to temptation, the more completely is it deprived of strength to resist them from without. Thus it is weakened still further at the very time when it is subjected to more violent attacks, and finally its internal support is removed, which, while it served as a refuse and asylum, would be an evidence of the goodness of God, and of its faithfulness to itself.

So you may see a man pursued by a powerful adversary; he fights and defends himself as well as he is able, always contriving, however, to get nearer and nearer to a stronghold of safety. But the longer he fights, the weaker he becomes, while the strength of his opponent is constantly increasing. What should he do? He will gain the portal of the stronghold as adroitly as he can, for there he will find abundant aid. But on reaching it, he sees that it is closed and finds that, far from rendering him any assistance, the keepers have barricaded every loophole of refuge. He must fall into the hands of his powerful enemy, whom he recognizes—when, defenseless and in despair, he has given himself up—as his best and truest friend.

Be sure, then, that this degree comprehends all these things—the privation of every good, the accumulation of all sorts of weaknesses, powerlessness of defense, no interior asylum, a God who Himself often appears angry, and, to crown all, temptations.

"Willingly," I think I hear you say, "provided I might be sure that my will was not in harmony with the malignity of nature and the weaknesses of the senses." Ah, you would be too happy, but that cannot be. In proportion as you become enfeebled and destitute of every operation and activity of love, however insignificant, the will, which was founded in that vigor of love, becoming weaker day by day, gradually disappears. And vanishing thus, it is certain that it takes no part in anything that is passing in the man but is separate. But as it does not manifest itself anywhere, by any sign, it affords no assured support to the soul, but the contrary. For no longer finding the will in an attitude of resistance, the soul believes that it is consenting to everything and that it has joined in with the animal will, which is the only one perceptible.

You will, perhaps, remind one that I have before stated that, in the first contest of amorous activity, nature and the senses had become, as it were, extinguished and subdued. It is true. But the spirit of self, by the very victories that grace had thus acquired for it, has become high-minded, more tenacious of what it esteems good and still more indomitable. God, who is determined to subdue it, makes use for that purpose, of an apparent resurrection of that same nature that the soul supposed dead. But observe that He does not use nature until He has extracted its malignity, destroyed it, and separated the superior will from that which rendered it violent and criminal. He extracts the venom of the viper and then uses it as an antidote to the spirit. Whoever will become acquainted with the admirable economy of grace and the wisdom of God in bringing man to a total sacrifice of self will be filled with delight and, insensible as he may be, will expire with love. The little traces of it that have been revealed to my heart have often overwhelmed me with ecstasy and transport.

Fidelity in this degree requires us to suffer spoliation to the whole extent of the designs of God without being anxious about ourselves, sacrificing to God all our interests both for time and for eternity. Nothing must be made a pretext for reserving or retaining the slightest atom, for the least reservation is the cause of an irreparable loss, as it prevents our death from being total. We must let God work His absolute pleasure and allow the winds and tempests to beat upon us from every quarter, submerged, as we may often be, beneath the tumultuous billows.

A wonderful thing is here perceived. Far from being estranged by our suffering and wretched state, it is then that God appears, and if any weakness has been apparent, He gives us some token of His immediate presence, as if to assure the soul for a moment that He was with it in its tribulation. I say for a moment, for it is of no service subsequently, as a support, but is rather intended to point out the way and invite the soul to the further loss of self.

These states are not continuous in their violence; there are remissions, which, while they afford space for taking breath, serve, at the same time, to render the subsequent trial more painful. For nature will make use of anything to sustain its life, as a drowning man will support himself in the water by clinging to the blade of a razor, without adverting to the pain it causes him, if there be nothing else within his reach.

5

The Fifth Degree: Mystical Death

Attacked thus on all sides by so many enemies, without life and without support, we have no resource but to expire in the arms of love. When death is complete, the most terrible states cause no further trouble. We do not recognize death from the fact of having passed through all these states, but by an absolute want of power to feel pain or to think of or care for self, and by our indifference to remaining there forever without manifesting the slightest sign of vitality. Life is evidenced by a will for or a repugnance to something, but here in this death of the soul, all things are alike. It remains dead and insensible to everything that concerns itself, and though God reduces it to what extremity He will, it feels no repugnance. It has no choice between being an angel or demon,[10] because it no longer has any eyes for self. It is then that God has placed all its enemies beneath His footstool and, reigning supreme, takes and possesses it the more fully as it has the more completely deserted itself. But this takes place by degrees.

There remains for a long time, even after death, a trace of the living heat, which is only gradually dissipated. All states effect

10. Note from the editor: That is, from any selfish consideration of its own position, it only wills what God wills for it, and if it were a supposable case that God should desire it to be a devil, that would be the very thing it would crave above all others. If there should be any minds, however, so constituted as not to be able to take in a supposition apparently so contrary to the revealed order of God, as we perceive it in His word and works—to such, it is an unprofitable nicety, which they may pass without concern.

somewhat toward cleansing the soul, but here the process is completed.

We do not die spiritually, once and for all, as we do naturally; it is accomplished gradually. We vibrate between life and death, being sometimes in one and sometimes in the other, until death has finally conquered life. And so it is in the resurrection—an alternate state of life and death until life has finally overcome death.

Not that the new life does not come suddenly. He who was dead finds himself living, and can never afterward doubt that he was dead and is alive again. But it is not then established. It is rather a disposition toward living than a settled state of life.

The first life of grace began in the sensible and sank continually inward toward the center, until, having reduced the soul to unity, it caused it to expire in the arms of love, for all experience this death, but each by means peculiar to himself. But the life that is now communicated arises from within. It is, as it were, a living germ that has always existed there, though unobserved, and which demonstrates that the life of grace has never been wholly absent, however it may have been allowed to remain hidden. There it remained even in the midst of death, and it was not less death because life was concealed in it, as the silkworm lies long dead in the chrysalis but contains a germ of life that awakes it to a resurrection. This new life, then, buds in the center and grows from there. Thence it gradually extends over all the faculties and senses, impregnating them with its own life and fecundity.

The soul, endued with this vitality, experiences an infinite contentment, not in itself, but in God, and this especially when the life is well advanced.

But before entering upon the effects of this admirable life, let me say that there are some who do not pass through these painful deaths; they only experience a mortal languor and fainting, which annihilate them and cause them to die to all.

Many spiritual persons have given the name of death to the earlier purifications, which are, indeed, a death in relation to the life communicated, but not a total death. They result in an extinguishment of some one of the lives of nature, or of grace, but that is widely different from a general extinction of all life.

Death has various names, according to our different manner of expression or conception. It is called a departure, that is, a separation from self in order that we may pass into God. It is called a loss, total and entire, of the will of the creature, which causes the soul to be wanting to itself so that it may exist only in God. Now, as this will is in everything that subsists in the creature, however good and holy it may be, all these things must necessarily be destroyed so far as they so subsist, and so far as the good will of man is in them, so that the will of God alone may remain. Everything born of the will of the flesh and the will of man must be destroyed. Then nothing but the will of God is left, which becomes the principle of the new life and, gradually animating the old extinguished will, takes its place and changes it into faith.

From the time that the soul expires mystically, it is separated generally from everything that would be an obstacle to its perfect union with God; but it is not, for all that, received into God. This causes it the most extreme suffering. You will object here that, if it be wholly dead, it can no longer suffer. Let me explain.

The soul is dead as soon as it is separated from self, but this death or mystic decease is not complete until it has passed into God. Until then, it suffers very greatly, but its suffering is general and indistinct and proceeds solely from the fact that it is not yet established in its proper place.

The suffering that precedes death is caused by our repugnance to the means that are to produce it. This repugnance to the means happens whenever these means recur or grow sharper. But as we die, we become more and more insensible and seem to harden under the blows until, at last, death comes in truth through an entire cessation of all life. God has unrelentingly pursued our life into all its covert hiding places. For so malignant is it that when hard pressed, it fortifies itself in its refuges and makes use of the holiest and most reasonable pretexts for existence. But being persecuted and followed into its last retreat, in a few souls (alas, how few!), it is obliged to abandon them altogether.

No pain then remains arising from the means that have caused our death and that are exactly the opposite to those that used to maintain our life. The more reasonable and holy the latter are in appearance, the more unreasonable and defiled is the look of the other.

But after death, which is the cause of the soul's departure from self—that is, of its losing every self-appropriation whatever (for we never know how strongly we cling to objects until they are taken away, and he who thinks that he is attached to nothing is frequently grandly mistaken, being bound to a thousand things, unknown to himself)—the soul is entirely rid of self, but not at first received into God. There still exists something; I know not exactly what—a form, a human remnant. But that also vanishes. It is a tarnish that is destroyed by a general, indistinct suffering, having no relation to the means of death, since they are passed away and completed. But it is an uneasiness arising from the fact of being turned out of self without being received into its great Original. The soul loses all possession of self, without which it could never be united to God, but it is only gradually that it becomes fully possessed of Him by means of the new life, which is wholly divine.

6

Union with God, but Not Yet Recognized

As soon as the soul has died in the embraces of the Lord, it is united to Him in truth and without any intermediate, for in losing everything, even its best possessions, it has lost the means and intermediates that dwelt in them. And even these greatest treasures themselves were but intermediates. It is, then, from that moment united to God immediately, but it does not recognize it, and it does not enjoy the fruits of its union until He animates it and becomes its vivifying principle. A bride fainting in the arms of her husband is closely united to him, but she does not enjoy the blessedness of the union and may even be unconscious of it. But when he has contemplated her for some time, fainting from excess of love, and recalls her to life by his tender caresses, then she perceives that she is in possession of him whom her soul loves, and that she is possessed by him.

Part II: On Union with God

1

The Resurrection

The soul thus possessed of God finds that He is so perfectly Lord over it that it can no longer do anything but what He pleases and as He pleases, and this state goes on increasing. Its powerlessness is no longer painful but pleasant, because it is full of the life and power of the divine will.

The dead soul is in union, but it does not enjoy the fruits of it until the moment of its resurrection, when God, causing it to pass into Him, gives it such pledges and assurances of the consummation of its divine marriage that it can no longer doubt. For this immediate union is so spiritual, so refined, so divine, so intimate that it is equally impossible for the soul to conceive or to doubt it. For we may observe that the whole way whereof we speak is infinitely removed from any imagination; these souls are not in the least imaginative, having nothing in the intellect, and they are perfectly protected from deceptions and illusions, as everything takes place within.

During their passage through the way of faith, they had nothing distinct, for distinctness is entirely opposed to faith, and they could not enjoy anything of that sort, having only a certain generality as a foundation upon which everything was communicated to them. But it is far otherwise when the life becomes advanced in God; for though they have nothing distinct for themselves, they have for others, and their illumination for the use of others, though not always received by those for whom it was intended, is the more certain as it is more immediate, and, as it were, natural.

When God raises a soul, that is to say, receives it into Himself, and the living germ, which is no other than the life and Spirit of the Word, begins to appear, it constitutes the revelation in it of Jesus Christ, who lives in us by the loss of the life of Adam subsisting in self.

The soul is thus received into God and is there gradually changed and transformed into Him, as food is transformed into the one who has partaken of it. All this takes place without any loss of its own individual existence, as has been elsewhere explained.

When transformation begins, it is called annihilation, since in changing our form, we become annihilated as to our own in order to take on His. This operation goes on constantly during life, changing the soul more and more into God and conferring upon it a continually increasing participation in the divine qualities, making it unchangeable, immovable, and so on. But He also renders it fruitful in, and not out of, Himself.

This fruitfulness extends to certain persons, whom God gives and attaches to the soul, communicating to it His love, full of charity. For the love of these divine souls for the persons, which is thus bestowed upon them, while it is far removed from the natural feelings, is infinitely stronger than the love of parents for their children, and though it appears eager and precipitate, it is not so, because he who exhibits it merely follows the movement impressed upon him.

To make this intelligible, we must know that God did not deprive the senses and faculties of their lives to leave them dead, for though there might be life in the center of the soul, they would remain dead if that life was not also communicated to them. It increases by degrees, animates all the powers and senses that (until then) had remained barren and unfruitful, enlarges them in proportion to its communication, and renders them active, but with an activity derived and regulated from God, according to His own designs. Persons in a dying or dead condition must not condemn the activity of such souls, for they could never have been put in divine motion if they had not passed through the most wonderful death. During the whole period of faith, the soul remains motionless, but after God has infused into it the divine activity, its sphere is vastly extended. But great as it may be, it cannot execute a self-originated movement.

2

The Life in God

There is no more to be said here of degrees; that of glory being all that remains, every means being left behind, and the future consisting in our enjoying an infinite stretch of life, and that more and more abundantly. (See John 10:10.) As God transforms the soul into Himself, His life is communicated to it more plentifully. The love of God for the creature is incomprehensible, and His assiduity inexplicable. Some souls He pursues without intermission; He seats Himself at their door and delights Himself in being with them and in loading them with the marks of His love. He impresses this chaste, pure, and tender love upon the heart. Saint Paul and Saint John the Evangelist felt the most of this maternal affection. But to be as I have described it, it must be bestowed upon the soul in the state of grace of which I have just spoken; otherwise, such emotions are purely natural.

The prayer of the state of faith is an absolute silence of all the powers of the soul and a cessation of every working, however delicate, especially toward its termination. The soul in that state, perceiving no more prayer and not being able to set apart fixed seasons for it, since all such exercises are taken away, is led to think that it has absolutely lost all kind of devotion. But when life returns, prayer returns with it and is accompanied by a marvelous facility. And as God takes possession of the senses and faculties, its devotion becomes sweet, gentle, and very spiritual, but always to God. Its former devotion caused it to sink within itself so that it might enjoy God, but that which it now has draws it out of self so that it may be more and more lost and changed in God.

This difference is quite remarkable and can only be accomplished by experience. The soul is silent in the state of death, but its stillness is barren and accompanied by a frantic rambling, which leaves no mark of silence save the impossibility of addressing God, either with the lips or the heart. But after the resurrection, its silence is fruitful and attended by an exceedingly pure and refined unction, which is deliciously diffused over the senses, but with such a purity that it occasions no stay and contracts no taint.

It is now impossible for the soul to take what it has not or to put off what it has. It receives with passive willingness whatever impressions are made upon it. Its state, however overwhelming, would be free from suffering if God, who moves it toward certain free things, gave them the necessary correspondence. But as their state will not bear it, it becomes necessary that God's will for what they should have needs to be communicated by means of suffering for them.

It would be wrong for such persons to say that they do not wish these means; that they desire God only. He is anxious that they should die to a certain interior support of self, which causes them to say that they desire God only, and if they were to reject these means, they would withdraw themselves from the order of God and arrest their progress. But being given simply as means, though fruitful in grace and virtue, however secret and concealed, they finally disappear when the soul finds itself united with the means in God, and He communicates Himself directly. Then God withdraws the means, upon which He no longer impresses any movement in the direction of the person to whom they are attached, because it might then serve as a stay, its utility being at least recognized. The soul can then no longer have what it had, and remains in its first death in respect to them, though still very closely united.

In this state of resurrection comes that ineffable silence, by which we not only subsist in God but commune with Him, and, in a soul thus dead to its own working and general and fundamental self-appropriation, it becomes a flux and reflux of divine communion, with nothing to sully its purity; for there is nothing to hinder it.

The soul then becomes a partaker of the ineffable communion of the Trinity, where the Father of spirits imparts His spiritual fecundity and makes it one spirit with Himself. Here it is that it communes with other souls, if they are sufficiently pure to receive its communications in silence, according to their degree and state. Here the ineffable secrets are revealed, not by a momentary illumination, but in God Himself, where they are all hidden, the soul not possessing them for itself or being ignorant of them.

Although I have said that the soul then has something distinct, yet it is not distinct in reference to itself but to those with whom it communes, for what it says is said naturally and without attention, but seems extraordinary to the hearers, who, not finding the thing in themselves, notwithstanding it may be there, consider it as something distinct and wonderful or perhaps fanatical. Souls who are still dwelling among the gifts have distinct and momentary illuminations, but these latter have only a general illumination without defined beams, which is God Himself. From Him they draw whatever they need, which is distinct whenever it is required by those with whom they are conversing, and without any of it remaining with themselves afterward.

3

The Transformation

There are a thousand things that might be said about the inward and celestial life of the soul thus full of life in God, which He dearly cherishes for Himself and which He covers externally with abasement because He is a jealous God. But it would require a volume, and I have only to fulfill your request. God is the life and soul of this soul, which thus uninterruptedly lives in God as a fish lives in the sea, in inexpressible happiness, though loaded with the sufferings that God lays upon it for others.

It has become so simple, especially when its transformation is far advanced, that it goes its way perpetually without a thought for any creature or for itself. It has but one object, to do the will of God. But as it has to do with many of the creatures who cannot attain to this state, some of them cause it suffering by endeavoring to compel it to have a care for self—to take precautions, and so on—which it cannot do; and others cause suffering by their want of correspondence to the will of God.

The crosses of such souls are the most severe, and God keeps them under the most abject humiliations and a very common and feeble exterior, though they are His delight. Then Jesus Christ communicates Himself in all His states, and the soul is clothed upon both with His inclinations and sufferings. It understands what man has cost Him, what his faithlessness has made Him suffer, what the redemption of Jesus Christ is, and how He has borne His children.

The transformation is recognized by the want of distinction between God and the soul, which is being able any longer to separate itself from God. Everything is equally God, because it has passed into its original Source, is reunited to its All , and is changed into Him. But it is enough for me to sketch the general outlines of what you desire to know; experience will teach you the rest, and having shown you what I ought to be to you, you may judge of what I am in our Lord.

As its transformation is perfected, the soul finds a more extended quality in itself. Everything is expanded and dilated, God making it a partaker of His infinity, so that it often finds itself immense, and the whole earth appears but as a point in comparison with this wonderful breadth and extension. Whatever is in the order and will of God expands it; everything else contracts it, and this contraction restrains it from passing out. As the will is the means of effecting the transformation, and the center is nothing else but all the faculties united in the will, the more the soul is transformed, the more its will is changed and passed into that of God, and the more God Himself wills for the soul. The soul acts and works in this divine will, which is thus substituted for its own, so naturally that it cannot tell whether the will of the soul has become the will of God, or the will of God has become the will of the soul.

God frequently exacts strange sacrifices from souls thus transformed in Him, but it costs them nothing, for they will sacrifice everything to Him without repugnance. The smaller sacrifices cost the most and the greater ones the least, for they are not required until the soul is in a state to grant them without difficulty, to which it has a natural tendency. This is what is said of Jesus Christ on His coming into the world: "*Then said I, Lo, I come: in the volume of the book it is written of me, I delight to do thy will, O my God: yea, thy law is within my heart*" (Psalm 40:7–8). As soon as Christ comes into any soul to become its living principle, He says the same thing of it; He becomes the eternal priest who unceasingly fulfills within the soul His sacerdotal office. This is sublime indeed and continues until the victim is carried to glory.

God destines these souls for the assistance of others in the most tangled paths, for since they no longer have any anxiety in regard to themselves or anything to lose, God can use them to bring others into the way of His pure, naked, and assured will. Those who are still self-possessed could not be used for this purpose, for, not having yet entered into a state where they follow the will of God blindly for themselves, but always mingling it with their own reasoning and false wisdom, they are not by any means in a condition to withhold nothing in following it blindly for others. When I say withhold nothing, I mean of that which God desires in the present moment, for He frequently does not permit us to point out to a person all that hinders him; and what we see must come to pass in respect to him, except in general terms, because he cannot bear it. And though we may sometimes say hard things, as Christ did to the people of Capernaum, He nevertheless bestows a secret strength to bear it. At least He does so to the souls whom He has chosen solely for Himself, and this is the touchstone.

SPIRITUAL MAXIMS

Attributed to Père Lacombe,
at one time a spiritual director of Madame Guyon

"Whom shall he teach knowledge? and whom shall he make to understand doctrine? them that are weaned from the milk, and drawn from the breasts."

—Isaiah 28:9

TO ROB GOD of nothing, to refuse Him nothing, to require of Him nothing—this is great perfection.[11]

IN THE COMMENCEMENT of the spiritual life, our hardest task is to bear with our neighbor in its progress with ourselves and in its end with God.

HE THAT REGARDS self only with horror is beginning to be the delight of God.

THE MORE WE learn what humility is, the less we discover of it in ourselves.

WHEN WE SUFFER aridity and desolation with equanimity, we testify our love to God, but when He visits us with the sweetness of His presence, He testifies His love to us.

---

11. Note from the editor: To appropriate nothing to ourselves, either of God's grace or glory, but to refer it all to Him; to yield up everything to Him with a cheerful and delighted heart the moment He asks for it; and to be so absolutely content with His will as to be able to confine our petitions to the simple prayer, "Your will be done," which, in truth, contains all prayer—this is, indeed, great perfection!

HE THAT BEARS the privations of the gifts of God and the esteem of men, with an even soul, knows how to enjoy His supreme good beyond all time and above all means.

LET NO ONE ask a stronger mark of an excellent love to God than that we are insensible to our own reputation.

WOULD YOU EXERT all your powers to attain divine Union? Use all your strength for the destruction of self. Be so much the enemy of self as you desire to be the friend of God.

HOW ARE WE directed in the law to love ourselves? In God, with the same love that we bear to God, because as our true selves are in Him, our love must be there also.

IT IS A rare gift to discover an indescribable something, which is above grace and nature, and which is not God, but which suffers no intermediate between God and us. It is a pure and unmixed emanation of a created being who is immediately connected with the uncreated Original, from whom he proceeds. It is a union of essence with essence, in which nothing that is neither can act the part of an intermediate.

THE RAY OF the creature is derived from the Sun of the Divinity. It cannot be separated from it, and if its dependence upon its divine principle is essential, its union is not less so. O wonder! The creature that can only be by the power of God cannot exist without Him, and, at the root of his being, nothing can come between or cause the slightest separation between God and him. This is the common condition of all creatures, but it is only perceived by those whose purified faculties can trace the grandeur of their center, and whose interior, freed from the defilement that covered it, begins to return to its origin.

FAITH AND THE cross are inseparable: The cross is the shrine of faith, and faith is the light of the cross.

IT IS ONLY by the death of self that the soul can enter into divine truth and understand in part what is the light that shines in darkness. And the more the darkness of self-knowledge deepens about us, the more the divine truth shines in our midst.

NOTHING LESS THAN a divine operation can empty us of the creature and of self, for whatever is natural tends constantly to fill us with the creature and occupy us with ourselves. This emptiness without anything distinct is, then, an excellent sign, though it exists surrounded by the deepest and (I may say) the most importunate temptations.

GOD CAUSES US to promise in time of peace what He exacts from us in time of war; He enables us to make our abandonments in joy, but He requires the fulfillment of them in the midst of much bitterness. It is well for You, O Love, to exercise Your rights; suffer as we may, we will not return to self, or if we suffer because we have done so, the remedy for the evil is to devote ourselves afresh with an enlarged abandonment. Strange malady, the cure of which is only to be found in a worse! O Lord, cause me to do whatever You want, provided I do only Your will.[12]

HOW HIDDEN IS the theology of love! O Love, You sully to excess what You would raise to the heights of purity! You profane Your own sanctuary; there is not left one stone upon another that is not cast into the dirt. And what will be the end? You know it from the beginning; it is worthy of so great a Workman that His work should be hidden, and that, while He seems to destroy, He should accomplish it the most effectually.

AH LORD, WHO sees the secrets of the heart, You know if I yet expect anything from myself or if there be anything that I would refuse to surrender to You! How rare is it to behold a soul in an absolute abandonment of selfish interests, that it may devote itself to the interests of God!

THE CREATURE WOULD willingly cease to be creature if it could become God, but where will we find one willing that God

12. Note from the editor: A proviso that the truly abandoned soul will not find necessary or rest easy under.

should resume everything He has bestowed without receiving anything in return? I say everything, and everything without reserve, even to our own righteousness, which is dearer to man than his existence, and to our rest, by which we enjoy self and the gifts of God in self, and in which we place our happiness without knowing it. Where will we find an abandonment that is as comprehensive as the will of God, not only when accompanied by delights, illumination, and feeling, but under all circumstances and in fact? O it is a fruit of Paradise that can scarce be found upon the earth!

GOD IS INFINITELY more honored by the sacrifices of death than by those of life. In the latter we honor Him as a great Sovereign; in the former, as God, losing all things for His glory. This is the reason why Jesus Christ made many more sacrifices of death than of life, and I suspect no one will gain all without having lost all.

REASON SHOULD NOT undertake to comprehend the last destructions; they are ordained expressly to destroy our reason.

GOD HAS MEANS more efficient, more conducive to His own glory, and more edifying for souls, but they are less sanctifying. These great and dazzling gifts are very gratifying to nature, even when it seems to give way beneath their weight, and thus nourish its secret life; but distresses, continual dying, and unprofitableness for any good crucify the most vital parts of the soul, which are those that prevent the coming of the kingdom of God.

IN OUR SOLEMN feasts, some strive to do something for You, O my God, and others strive that You may do something for them, but neither of these is permitted to us. Love forbids the one and cannot suffer the other.

IT IS HARDER to die to our virtues than to our vices, but the one is just as necessary as the other for perfect union. Our attachments are the stronger as they are more spiritual.

WHAT IS A help to perfection at one time is a hindrance at another; what formerly helped you in your way to God will now prevent you from reaching Him. The more wants we have, the further we are from God, and the nearer we approach Him, the better can we dispense with everything that is not Himself. When we have come there, we use everything indifferently and have no more need but of Him.

WHO CAN SAY to what extent the divine abandonment will carry the poor soul that is given up to it? Or rather, to whom can we describe the extremity of sacrifice that God exacts from His simple victim? He raises him by degrees and then plunges him into the abyss; he discovers new points to him day by day and never ceases until he has sacrificed everything God wills, putting no other bounds to his abandonment than God does to His decrees. He even goes further, submitting to everything that God could do or His sovereign will ordain. Then every selfish interest is given up; all is surrendered to the Author of all, and God reigns supreme over his nothingness.

GOD GIVES US gifts, graces, and natural talents, not for our own use, but so that we may render them to Him. He takes pleasure in giving and in taking them away or in so disposing of us that we cannot enjoy them; but their grand use is to be offered in a continual sacrifice to Him, and by this, He is most glorified. Naked faith keeps us in ignorance, uncertainty, and oblivion of everything in reference to ourselves. It says everything, excepting nothing, neither grace nor nature, virtue nor vice. It is the darkness concealing us wholly from ourselves but revealing so much the more of the Divinity and the greatness of His works—an obscurity that gives us an admirable discernment of spirits and dislodges the esteem and love of self from its most secret recesses. Pure love reigns underneath, notwithstanding. For how can a soul go about to consider its own interest when it cannot as much as look at itself? Or how could it be pleased to look at what it cannot see? It either sees nothing or nothing but God, who is all and in all; and the more it is blinded to self, the more it beholds of Him.

THERE ARE BUT few men who are led by their reason; most of them are fewer, indeed, who act from an illuminated faith or from reason enlightened by faith. But will we find a single one who admits no guide but a blind faith, which, though it leads him straight to God by the short road of abandonment, seems, nevertheless, to precipitate him into abysses from which he has no hope of ever escaping? There are, however, some such souls who have noble trust enough to be blindfolded and led they know not where. Many are called, but few are willing to enter, and those who have most fully surrendered themselves to the sway of their senses, their passions, their reason, and the distinct illuminations of faith are those who have the greatest difficulty plunging into the gulf of the blindest and most naked faith. By contrast, the simple souls enter with ease. It is the same as with the shipwrecked. Those who know how to swim, or who have perhaps seized a plank of the ship, struggle and contend for a long while before they drown. But those who cannot swim and who have nothing to sustain them are instantly submerged and, sinking without a struggle beneath the surface, die and are delivered from their suffering.

THE SPIRITUALITY OF most spiritual persons is nothing but presumption. When the divine Truth penetrates to their center, it discovers many a theft from God in their course, and teaches them that the only way to secure themselves is by abandonment without reserve to God and submission to His guidance. For whenever we endeavor to bring about our own perfection or that of others, by our own efforts, the result is simply imperfection. It is in vain for man to endeavor to instruct man in those things that the Holy Spirit alone can teach.

THE SOUL THAT is destined to have no other support but God Himself must pass through the strangest trials. How much agony and how many deaths must it suffer before losing the life of self! It will encounter no purgatory in the other world, but it will feel a terrible hell in this, a hell not only of pain—that would be a small matter—but also of temptations its own resistance to which it does not perceive. This is the cross of crosses, of all sufferings the most intolerable, of all deaths the most despairing.

ALL CONSOLATION THAT does not come from God is but desolation; when the soul has learned to receive no comfort but in God only, it has passed beyond the reach of desolation. By the alternations of interior union and desertion, God sometimes makes us feel what He is, and sometimes gives us to perceive what we are. He does the latter to make us hate and die to ourselves, but the former to make us love Him and to exalt us into union.

TO TAKE AND receive all things not in ourselves, but in God, is the true and excellent way of dying to ourselves and living only to God. Those who understand the practice of this are beginning to live purely, but outside of this, nature is always mingled with grace, and we rest in self instead of permitting ourselves no repose, except in the Supreme Good, who should be the center of every movement of the heart as He is the final end of all the measures of love.

WHY SHOULD WE complain that we have been stripped of the divine virtues if we had not hidden them away as our own? Why should we complain of a loss if we had no property in the thing lost? Or why does deprivation give us so much pain, except because of the appropriation we had made of that which was taken away?

O MONSTER JUSTLY abhorred of God and man, after being humiliated in so many ways, I cannot become humble, and I am so pampered with pride that when I most endeavor to be humble, I set about my own praises! When you cannot find yourself, or any good, then rejoice that all things are rendered unto God.

SOME SAINTS HAVE been sanctified by the easy and determined practice of all the virtues, but there are others who owe their sanctification to having endured with perfect resignation the privation of every virtue.

IF WE DO not go as far as to be stopped by nothing short of the power of God, we are not entirely free from presumption; and if our abandonment is bounded by anything short of the possible will of God, we are not yet disengaged from appropriation. And presumption and appropriation are impurities.

I HAVE NEVER found any who prayed as well as those who had never been taught how. Those who have no master in man have one in the Holy Spirit. He who has a pure heart will never cease to pray, and he who will be constant in prayer will know what it is to have a pure heart.

GOD IS SO great and so independent that He can find means to glorify Himself even by sin.

WHILE OUR ABANDONMENT blesses or spares us, we will find many to advise it; but let it bring us into trouble, and the most spiritually minded ones will exclaim against it.

IT IS EASY enough to understand the course of such as go on from virtue to virtue, but who can comprehend the decrees that send some dashing from one precipice to another and from one abyss to another? Or who will bring aid and comfort to these hidden favorites of God, whom He gradually deprives of every stay, and whom are reduced to an inability to know or help themselves, as utter as their ignorance of what sustains them?

WHO CAN COMPREHEND the extent of that supreme homage that is due to the will of God?

THOSE WHO ARE abandoned are cast from one precipice to another and from one abyss to another as if they were lost.

THE HARMLESSNESS OF the dove consists in not judging another; the wisdom of the serpent in distrusting ourselves.

SELF-SEEKING IS the gate by which a soul departs from peace, and total abandonment to the will of God is that by which it returns.

ALAS, HOW HARD it is to will only the will of God and yet to believe that we do nothing but what is contrary to that will! To desire nothing so much as to do His will and not even to know what it is! To be able to show it with great confidence to others but not to find it for ourselves! When we are full of His will, and everywhere penetrated by it, we no longer know it. This is, indeed, a long and painful martyrdom, but one that will result in an unchangeable peace in this life and an incomprehensible felicity in the next!

HE WHO HAS learned to seek nothing but the will of God will always find what he seeks.

WHICH IS THE harder lot for a soul that has known and loved God, not to know whether it loves God or whether God loves it?

WHICH OF THE two would the perfect soul choose, if the choice were presented—to love God or to be loved by Him?

TELL ME, WHAT is that which is neither separated from God nor united to God, but which is inseparable from Him?

WHAT IS THE state of a soul that has neither power nor will? And what can it do and not do?

WHO WILL MEASURE the extent of the abandonment of a soul that is no longer self-possessed in anything, and that has an absorbing sense of the supremacy of the power and will of God?

WHO CAN TAKE in the extent of the interior sacrifices of Jesus Christ, except the one to whom He will manifest them?

HOW CAN THEY who are not willing to abandon all their possessions be delivered from the life of self?

HOW CAN THEY who possess the greatest treasure under heaven believe themselves despoiled of all? Do not oblige me to name it, but judge, if you are enlightened; there is one of them that is less than the other, that is lost before it, but that those who must lose everything have the greatest trouble in parting with.

About the Authors

François Fénelon (1651–1715) was the archbishop of Cambrai. He met Christian contemplative Madame Jeanne Guyon in 1688, apparently appreciating and affirming some of her doctrines and contemplative practices but on other occasions distancing himself from them. In 1689, he was appointed tutor to the grandson of Louis XIV. He became archbishop in 1695. Fénelon wrote letters of spiritual counsel that are highly valued to this day.

Jeanne Guyon (1648–1717) wrote from the depth of her own spiritual experiences. Growing up in France during the decadent times of Louis XIV, she was devout at an early age but was then caught up in the worldliness around her. After an arranged marriage at the age of fifteen, she became increasingly interested in spiritual things; and, for the rest of her life, she continued to seek God diligently. She also began to teach others and write books on Christian devotion. Many of these books have become Christian classics. Guyon paid a heavy price for some of her views and her writings. Throughout her life, she underwent various trials, including persecution and imprisonment for her beliefs. Her commentary on Song of Solomon was used to sentence her to prison.

Very little is known about Père Lacombe (1643–1713), other than that he was a Barnabite priest who mentored Madame Guyon. Lacombe guided Guyon along a series of "interior experiences." Under his spiritual guidance, Guyon was able to go from a deep sense of God's presence to a "mystical death," and then to a state in which she no longer possessed God but He possessed her. It was this experience that led Guyon to write *A Short and Easy Method of Prayer* in 1685. In 1686, King Louis XIV ordered that Lacombe, who had publicly defended Guyon, be imprisoned in the Bastille and afterward in the castles of Oloron and of Lourdes.